MULTINATIONAL JOINT VENTURES IN DEVELOPING COUNTRIES

INTERNATIONAL BUSINESS SERIES

Academic Editor: Alan M. Rugman, University of Toronto

MULTINATIONAL JOINT VENTURES
IN
DEVELOPING COUNTRIES

Paul W. Beamish

ʀ

ROUTLEDGE
London and New York

First published 1988
by Routledge
11 New Fetter Lane, London EC4P 4EE
29 West 35th Street, New York, NY 10001
Reprinted 1989

© 1988 Paul W. Beamish

Typeset by Pat and Anne Murphy,
Highcliffe-on-Sea, Dorset.

Printed in Great Britain by
Antony Rowe Ltd, Chippenham, Wiltshire

British Library Cataloguing in Publication Data

Beamish, Paul W.
  Multinational joint ventures in developing
  countries. — (Routledge series in
  international business).
  1. International business enterprises —
  Developing countries 2. Joint ventures —
  Developing countries
  I. Title II. Series
  338.8′881724 HD2932
  ISBN 0-415-00394-6

Library of Congress Cataloging in Publication Data

Beamish, Paul W., 1953-
  Multinational joint ventures in developing countries.

  (The Routledge series in international business)
  Bibliography: p.
  Includes index.
  1. International business enterprises—Developing
  countries. 2. Joint ventures—Developing countries.
  I. Title. II. Series.
  HD2932.B43 1988   338.8′881724   88-6445
  ISBN 0-415-00394-6

Contents

Tables

To my parents,
John Richard Beamish
and
Catherine Margaret Beamish

Preface

True to the spirit of joint venturing, this book is a collaborative effort in many respects. Half of the chapters are based on articles written with five different colleagues — Henry W. Lane at the University of Western Ontario, Jean-Louis Schaan at the University of Ottawa, John C. Banks at Wilfrid Laurier University, Hui Wang from the People's Republic of China and Terrance W. Conley at the Toronto Law firm of Blake, Cassels and Graydon. These joint efforts, plus those chapters which I wrote alone, have been updated since their original publication. All the material is post-1985.

Integrating the articles into a coherent chapter format did not present major problems thanks to word processing technology and Elsie Grogan, Susan Kirkey and Maureen Nordin.

The first draft of a portion of this book was my dissertation, completed in 1984. I am well aware that when many people finally finish their dissertations, the last thing they want to write about or research further is their thesis topic. This was not the case for me. When Alan Rugman (now at the University of Toronto) approached me in 1984 about writing a book on joint ventures, I was enthused. As Chapter 1 notes, JVs are an organisational form whose time has come — and for many good reasons.

Having worked in the area of joint ventures for over five years, I have received much useful assistance and direction. In addition to help from my co-authors, Tom Poynter (now at MIT) provided feedback on endless early versions of much of the material. That he did this without complaint, speaks highly of his patience. Louis T. Wells at Harvard provided suggestions on organising the early materials, and was the first to point me in the direction of tying my work to the theory of the MNE.

Peter Killing has been a source of constant encouragement ever since I 'mentioned' more than a decade ago, my possible interest in graduate studies. His work serves as an important reference point, both to myself and to many other joint venture researchers. In my view, this present book on MNE joint ventures in LDCs could serve as a companion text to his book *Strategies for Joint Venture Success*, which focused on MNE joint ventures in developed countries.

Executives in Canada, the United States, the United Kingdom and several Caribbean countries were unstinting in the amount of time they allowed to discuss joint ventures. The list of executives is both too long to note here and would in some instances violate their preference for confidentiality. Nonetheless, I would like to acknowledge the help of three individuals in particular, who were paid more than one visit — Bill Shurniak from CIBC (now at Hutchison-Whampoa), Richard Gould from Canada Wire and Cable, and Ken Boyea from Maple Leaf Mills. In many ways, the co-authors of this book could well be the nearly 100 managers with whom I have discussed joint ventures.

Financial support was provided by the Plan for Excellence and the Centre for International Business Studies, School of Business Administration, University of Western Ontario. As well, Wilfrid Laurier University provided travel support which enabled me to present earlier drafts of some of these chapters at conferences and meetings in Canada, the United States, Europe and Hong Kong.

My wife Maureen 'kept the home fires burning' at the expense of her own career whenever I was away. I am grateful for this. Finally, this book is dedicated to my parents, John and Catherine Beamish who, by example, have always urged me to persevere in any worthwhile endeavours.

London and Waterloo
Ontario, Canada
Paul W. Beamish

1

Introduction

1.1 IMPORTANCE OF JOINT VENTURES

Joint ventures, not wholly-owned subsidiaries, are the dominant form of business organisation for multinational enterprises (MNEs) in less developed countries (LDCs) (Vaupel and Curhan, 1973), and are frequently being used by Fortune 500 companies in the developed countries (Harrigan, 1985). In fact, for US-based companies, all cooperative arrangements (involving such things as licences or local shareholders) outnumber wholly-owned subsidiaries by a ratio of four to one (Contractor and Lorange, 1987).

The number of joint ventures is growing worldwide at an increasing pace. *Mergers and Acquisitions* (1983) reported a 59 per cent increase between 1981 and 1983 in the number of international joint ventures involving US firms. Active joint venturers include General Motors, Dana, Eaton, Beatrice, Pillsbury, Carnation, Borden and Control Data Corporation. Besides being major players in their respective industries, each operates anywhere from five to 20 joint ventures in developing countries. And these are not just any type of joint venture — in none of the 71 LDC-based joint ventures of these eight American firms do they have a majority equity interest (Franko, 1986).

Yet, given the relative importance of joint ventures in LDCs, it is surprising to find a negligible amount of research into ways of improving their performance. This is particularly significant since the limited literature on joint ventures suggests that performance problems are more acute in developing rather than

1

developed countries (Janger, 1980; and Franko, 1976). Over 100 nations are classified as developing countries. These potential markets are too big to ignore. For example, total GNP for Brazil exceeds that of Canada, or Norway, Sweden, Denmark and Finland combined; Nigeria's GNP exceeds that of Austria; Mexico's GNP exceeds that of Switzerland (Matthews and Morrow, 1985). Japanese and North American companies are not ignoring them. Existing and potential investment in these countries is substantial. Knowing how to operate successfully in these countries can be a problem, however.

The purpose of this research is to address the question of how the performance of joint business ventures in developing countries can be improved. Frequent performance problems of joint ventures in LDCs are an important issue for both MNE and host-country interests. Performance difficulties are costly for the MNE in time and capital. In addition, although the research does not emphasise it, there are also social costs to the host country when joint ventures experience difficulties or fail (Casson, 1979).

Organisations such as the United States Agency for International Development, the Canadian International Development Agency (CIDA) and the World Bank have recently been encouraging greater private sector involvement in developing countries. Much of the focus of the development agencies has been on the use of joint ventures, since joint ventures are a proven mechanism for transferring technology from the industrialised countries to LDCs. Not surprisingly, a number of government programmes have been established to assist in setting up joint ventures in LDCs. For example in Canada, CIDA activities have included the publication of a guide on how to establish a successful international joint venture, and the setting up of an industrial cooperation programme to assist financially in the promotion of mutually profitable business relationships between Canadian companies and their developing country counterparts.

By creating viable joint ventures in LDCs, international development can be speeded up. However, given the declining share of direct investment flows from the industrialised countries to LDCs (Robock and Simmonds, 1983), the costs of joint venture failure in LDCs are magnified.

Other researchers have independently examined joint ventures in developing countries, joint ventures in developed countries, and joint-venture performance. This research combines several of these elements by focusing in depth on the performance of joint ventures in developing countries. (The distinction used for developed/less developed countries is: 1978 *per capita* GNP over/under US $3,000. Based on World Bank figures, nearly three-quarters of the world's nations would be classed as LDCs.) In this research, joint ventures are defined as shared-equity undertakings between two or more parties, each of which holds at least five per cent of the equity. The research is concerned with joint ventures that have been formed between a company, group or individual from a developed country with a similar entity in a less developed country. While such groups can and do include local governments as partners, the focus of the research is on joint ventures in which the local government is not a shareholder. None of the core ventures involves government partners. The importance of focusing on this particular form of foreign equity investment is supported by recent research on US multinational enterprises in developing countries: 'Both US MNEs and host-country executives believe that a joint venture with a private local firm offers more advantages when compared with any other form of foreign equity investment for the US MNE and the host country' (Raveed and Renforth, 1983). Inclusion in the study required that the venture be in manufacturing (rather than services, mining or distribution) and to have been in operation for at least three years (whether it still operated or not). Non-manufacturing ventures are excluded because mixing joint ventures in a sample where the scale of investment is commonly much higher (mining) or lower (distribution) could potentially affect the joint-venture decision process. Because many joint ventures never get off the ground, those firms which had been fully operating businesses for less than three years are also excluded, to increase the comparability of the sample.

The most common partner for MNEs in LDCs is a local private firm. Other partner combinations are not included in the sample because they are either not typical (i.e. two MNE partners in an LDC) or because the partners might not share the same profit motivation (i.e. government partners being more concerned with employment than profitability). Also excluded from the study are one-shot, project-oriented ventures (sometimes known as fade-out joint ventures) and ventures in which the parent company views its involvement principally as a portfolio-like investment.

Incorporated into this research are modifications to other

3

researchers' methodologies and emphases. For example, previously used proxies for joint-venture performance, such as stability, are improved upon, and emphasis is extended beyond the more common examination of ownership/control influences on performance by introducing the concepts of joint need and commitment. In addition, these latter variables are related to performance using improved data collection and analysis procedures.

1.2 KEY VARIABLES

The largest part of this research investigates the effect on joint-venture performance of two variables to which other researchers have paid limited attention — need and commitment. It is hypothesised that greater need and commitment between partners results in more satisfactory performance.

Following a series of pilot-survey interviews, the potential impact of these variables upon performance emerged. In the subsequent focus on these variables, partner-need was assessed over a span of time in terms of the relative importance of each partner's contribution to the joint venture in a number of aspects such as capital, knowledge and staff. Joint-venture commitment was assessed in terms of the firm's commitment to international business, the joint-venture structure, the particular venture and the particular partner. Measures of need and commitment based on the early interviews and literature reviews are developed. The literature examined included both joint-venture and international business literature, and literature adapted from other disciplines such as organisational behaviour and management-information systems. These other disciplines are specifically examined for assistance in defining and measuring commitment. The need and commitment results are combined to form a managerial guideline for the establishment of successful joint ventures in LDCs.

The dependent variable — joint-venture performance — is defined according to whether there was mutual agreement between the partners regarding their overall satisfaction. The performance measure, with its basis in both partners' being satisfied, proved to be a better way of evaluating performance than the single-perspective measure used by other researchers, in which only the MNE partner's view is considered. Because partners sometimes differ in their assessment of performance, other measures of joint-venture performance are not as accurate. Emphasis on ensuring the long-term viability of the venture underlies the discussion of success in this research. Seven of the twelve core ventures classed as satisfactory performers use this system.

The research also investigates the effects of a number of independent variables, (e.g. ownership, control) considered important by researchers examining joint-venture performance primarily in developed countries. Investigation of their effect upon performance represents a replication of the work of other researchers, to some extent, although on what was considered to be a different population of joint ventures — those in developing countries.

1.3 OVERVIEW OF CONCLUSIONS

The principal conclusions of the research are noted below in the order in which they were derived. This order is also maintained in subsequent material — with the exception of the research methodology, presented in the section following. In considering methodology, the research question, the research design employed and the data collection process are detailed.

The first conclusion (Chapter 2) notes that characteristics of joint ventures in LDCs differ from those in developed countries. These characteristics — assessed in terms of stability, performance, ownership, reason for creating the venture, frequency of government partners and autonomy — were observed to differ following an analysis of, and comparison with, developed-country joint-venture samples.

This research suggests next that decision-making control in joint ventures in developing countries should be shared with the local partner, or split between the partners. There was support for the observation that there is a weakening of the link between joint-venture performance and the multinational having dominant management control, when one considers developing, rather than developed, countries.

Two important conclusions in Chapters 3 and 4 are that both partner need and commitment prove to be good predictors of both satisfactory and unsatisfactory joint-venture performance. For example, there is a positive association with performance of

MNEs using local management, being willing to use voluntarily the joint venture structure, and looking to the local partner for knowledge of the local economy, politics and customs.

In Chapter 5 a management guideline for implementing an existing or potential joint-venture strategy is provided. The data on which this chapter is based come from joint ventures in Latin America, Africa, Southeast Asia and the Caribbean region. The co-authors were able to interview both parties to the joint ventures and their general managers in a number of situations. The information was collected by a variety of means: experience, case research, structured interviews and questionnaires. Lane was involved in the formation of a joint venture in Africa and has conducted extensive case research on joint ventures and cross-cultural management in Latin America and Southeast Asia.

Chapter 6 examines the role of the joint venture general manager (JVGM). It draws extensively on Jean-Louis Schaan's original research on joint-venture control in Mexico. The JVGM plays a critical role in the successful operation on any joint venture, but has frequently been the forgotten person in joint-venture research.

Chapter 7 concludes that the joint-equity ventures do have a role in the theory of the multinational enterprise. With few exceptions, the theory has considered joint ventures as limited-term, contractual arrangements. As risky as joint ventures might be, there are conditions under which they are most appropriate for MNEs investing in foreign countries.

Chapters 8 and 9 look at joint ventures in a different group of developing countries, those with non-market economies. This study of joint ventures in China is based on new data, and lays particular emphasis on legal implications and the separating of fact from fiction regarding this market.

The appendices provide partial lists of firms contacted, as well as joint-venture management case studies.

1.4 METHODOLOGY

Data were collected by Beamish (1984) in three stages on a total of 66 joint ventures located in 27 LDCs. Within the third stage, particular emphasis was placed on twelve comparative core cases. Interviews were conducted with, and questionnaires administered to, the local partner, MNE partner, and joint-venture general manager (where possible) in each of these core ventures. This attempt to solicit information from both partners and the general manager for each venture represents a major point of departure from many previous works on joint-venture performance. This is important because it provides a more balanced picture of the actual operation of the joint venture and increased confidence in the research findings.

The questionnaires administered in the core ventures lent themselves to non-parametric statistical analysis of data. Although questionnaire findings from the twelve core ventures are emphasised, they are supplemented by interview comments from 46 senior executives in 66 joint ventures.

Table 1.1: Data collection

Data collection phases (number of interviews)	Joint ventures in the Caribbean countries	Joint ventures in non-Caribbean LDCs	Total number of joint ventures
1) Pilot survey (7)	3	31	34
2) Pre-test (12)	0	10	10
3) Test (27)	17	5	22[1]
Total (46)	20	46	66

Note: 1. Complete data (from all partners) were available for twelve of these ventures.

Interviews were conducted in five countries — Canada, the United States, the United Kingdom and two Caribbean nations. The 46 interviews averaged more than three hours in length each, and were, with five exceptions, conducted in person; the other five took place by telephone.

Over 100 executives were contacted in obtaining the 46 interviews. A larger original pool was required because of the need to find joint ventures that satisfied methodological constraints. Companies agreed to participate in the research in approximately 90 per cent of cases where the interviewer was able to establish that the companies' venture fitted the sample design. These core ventures were all between either American, British, or Canadian MNEs and local, private firms. Ten of the twelve joint ventures were located in the Caribbean, with most of these in a single country. The core ventures were concentrated in two sectors. There were both high- and low-performing ventures in each sector. Even though this required a longer search for companies, holding industry and country constant was considered an important step in reducing the number of rival explanations of joint-venture performance. All of the joint ventures in these industries were sampled. The research used structured interviews and a self-administered questionnaire. These questionnaires were administered with the researcher present so that questions could be immediately clarified. This also permitted the checking of responses to ensure consistency with comments made earlier in the interview.

The sample of joint ventures was not a random sample of the joint ventures in the region. A stratified sample of joint ventures between foreign private and local private firms, primarily in one country, was used.

Average sales for the venture were US $4.5 million, and all of the twelve ventures had sales between US $1 million and $10 million. There was no correlation between sales and performance. Five of the ventures sold to both industrial customers and consumers; two, to industrial customers only; and five, to consumers only. Half of the joint ventures exported, with no correlation between exporting and performance.

Average market share for the core ventures was 42 per cent, with a high standard deviation. There was no correlation between market share and joint-venture performance. The joint ventures were formed between 1959 and 1978 and had been in operation an average of 11.5 years. There was no correlation between age and performance.

None of the core ventures had effective monopoly positions. Either local manufacturing competition existed or tariffs were low enough to allow competitive import. The MNE held a minority equity share in five of the twelve ventures. Half of the core ventures exported (up to 25 per cent of sales), with no correlation between exporting and performance.

The basis for the measure of success used in this study was the long-term viability of the joint venture. Performance of the joint ventures was measured by a managerial assessment in which only when both partners were satisfied was the venture considered successful. If one or both partners were dissatisfied with the performance, the venture was considered unsuccessful. This measure was previously used in joint-venture research by Schaan (1983). In every case in which the venture was assessed by management as successful, both partners were also earning a 15 per cent or higher return on equity. Overall, seven of the twelve ventures were classed as successful and five as unsuccessful.

While it may be possible to operate a joint venture for a short period with a dissatisfied partner, refusing to recognise differences is ultimately costly in terms of the long-term viability of the JV. MNE partners who are satisfied with their own returns and yet ignore their partner's dissatisfaction with performance are ultimately sowing the seeds of destruction of the joint venture. Local partners will not tolerate unsatisfactory performance indefinitely, particularly if they perceive differences in the returns earned by the other partner. When the MNE partner had two sources of income (irrespective of type) additional to those of the local partner, poor performance resulted. When there was a closer balance in the numbers of sources of income for each partner, more satisfactory performance was observed. This is generally consistent with Contractor's (1985: 44) point that 'in some cases the optimum for the local partner is to try to disallow a royalty or component supply agreement altogether and negotiate only on an equity-sharing basis.'

If the MNE partner is satisfied or complacent about his own performance, and the local partner is not, the local partner has numerous ways in which to express dissatisfaction. If, for example, the local partner loses trust in the foreign partner (i.e. perceives that the MNE partner is operating opportunistically) he may move towards the formalisation or enforcement of various contracts surrounding the operations of the venture. As noted earlier, the costs of such actions would negate much of the rationale for the establishment of the joint venture in the first place.

2

Characteristics of Joint Ventures*

2.1 DEVELOPED VERSUS DEVELOPING COUNTRIES

In order to manage numerous foreign subsidiaries and affiliates, multinational enterprise (MNE) executives have sometimes given similar treatment to their joint ventures, wherever they were located. This has frequently resulted in serious performance problems. Why is it that all joint ventures cannot be managed the same way? As a partial explanation, this chapter argues that because environments differ, the rules of thumb which executives have derived from experiences in certain groups of countries will not be applicable in other locales.

The external environment influences both the initial configuration and the stability of a joint venture (Harrigan, 1984). Here, the external environment is considered to include such things as industry structure, competitive behaviour, technology and government policies.

The purpose of this chapter is to demonstrate that developed and developing countries represent different external environments; developing countries (LDCs) are considered a more complex and difficult environment to manage joint ventures in than that of developed countries. This chapter shows that certain characteristics of joint ventures differ between developed and developing countries and that joint ventures in LDCs are characterised by a higher instability rate and greater managerial dissatisfaction. The characteristics examined include reasons for creating the venture, autonomy, stability, performance, frequency of government partners and ownership. Particular emphasis is placed on ownership/control results and their relationship to performance because this has been the focus of most previous research attention.

The evidence to support these observations is based on the author's sample of joint ventures in LDCs (Chapter 1) and results from a dozen other empirical studies of joint ventures from both developed and developing countries. Not included are studies which look at joint ventures between firms from two third world countries (for example Wells, 1983).

2.2 VENTURE-CREATION RATIONALES

In a sample of 34 joint ventures in developed countries, Killing (1983) divides the reasons for creating a venture into three groups: (a) government suasion or legislation; (b) partner's needs for other partner's skills; and (c) partner's needs for the other partner's attributes or assets. Assets include such items as cash or patents, while attributes which make a firm desirable for joint venture purposes are the use or manufacture of certain products.

Table 2.1 illustrates how joint ventures are created for different reasons in developed and developing countries. Sixty-four per cent of the ventures in Killing's (1983) developed-country sample were created when each partner needed the other's skills. Only 38 per cent of the joint ventures in Beamish's (1984) LDC sample were created for this reason. The primary skill required by the MNE partner of the local firms was its knowledge of the local economy, politics and culture.

Table 2.1: Relationship of stage of development to venture-creation rationales

	Developed country %	LDC %
Government suasion or legislation	17	57
Skills needed	64	38
Assets or attribute needed	19	5

Nineteen per cent of the ventures in the developed country sample were created because one partner needed the other's attributes or assets. Only five per cent of the LDC sample were created for this reason.

Seventeen per cent of the ventures in the developed-country sample were created as the result of government suasion or legislation, whereas 57 per cent of joint ventures were created for this reason in LDCs. Janger (1980) obtained a similar result in LDCs, noting that nearly half of the companies in his sample that formed joint ventures did so as a result of government requirement. Gullander (1976) added that the one reason why many multinational firms, particularly in LDCs, would accept the joint-venture structure would be political. Tomlinson (1970) using a sample of joint ventures in India and Pakistan, also noted that the major reason for using joint-venture organisation was either explicit or implicit government pressures.

A common misconception is that countries either require the use of joint ventures or do not. In LDCs it is seldom this clear: a few LDCs require most companies to form joint ventures; while most LDCs require only a few companies, those in strategic sectors, to form joint ventures. In several firms surveyed the MNE realised after-the-fact that its early perception of being forced to form a joint venture by the local government was false.

Multinationals formed joint ventures for a variety of government-related reasons. These range from being legislated to become a joint venture to the multinational perceiving an advantage in attaining government contracts by having local ownership. A frequently occurring scenario was one where non-tariff barriers such as import restrictions were initiated to the extent that the multinational would lose his access to the market if he did not establish a local manufacturing facility.

A number of multinational companies establishing joint ventures in LDCs already had manufacturing facilities (usually wholly-owned subsidiaries) in the host company. Most frequently, the subsidiary was converted to a joint venture after serious problems were encountered in trying to do business in the local market.

2.3 STABILITY

A joint venture instability rate of 45 to 50 per cent was observed by both Beamish (1984) and by Reynolds (1979) in LDCs. This is consistently higher than the 30 per cent joint venture instability rate found by Killing (1983) and Franko (1971) in developed countries (see Table 2.2).

It bears noting again that we are dealing here only with ventures that have been in existence for at least three years. There are an enormous number of joint ventures where two partners sign an agreement but never actually proceed (Chapter 8); or where one or both partners back out shortly after some or all of the initial investment has been made. Not surprisingly, higher instability rates have been observed by those researchers (Kogut, 1987) who have included in their samples joint ventures in operation for less than three years.

The fact that there are so many false starts in the process of joint-venture formation provides additional impetus to find means of improving MNE joint-venture performance in LDCs.

Table 2.2: Relationship of stage of development to joint-venture instability and a managerial assessment of performance

Sample size	Development level of country	Unstable[1] %	Unsatisfactory performance %
1,100	Primarily developed (DC)		
	— Franko	30	—[2]
36	Developed (DC) — Killing	30[3]	36
168	Mixed (DC and LDC) — Janger	—[2]	37
60	Mixed (DC and LDC) — Stuckey	42[3]	—[2]
66	Developing — Beamish	45[3]	61
52	Developing — Reynolds	50	—[2]

Notes:
1. Franko defined a joint venture as unstable where (a) the holdings of the MNE crossed the 50 per cent or 95 per cent ownership lines, (b) the interests of the MNE were sold, or (c) the venture was liquidated.
2. No data provided.
3. Includes major reorganisations.

It was possible to compare the stability rates of joint ventures between foreign partners and both local government and local private partners (Table 2.3). Whether in mining (Stuckey, 1983) or manufacturing, those ventures involving government partners had an overall instability rate of 56 to 58 per cent. This was much higher than the 43 per cent instability rate of joint ventures between foreign and local private partners. Thus even when the more unstable government ventures are excluded from the LDC sample, it was still well above the developed-country level.

A possible influence on joint venture stability is the age of the

Table 2.3: Stability rates: government *vs.* private partners

| Samples | Government partner | | | Private partner | | | Total |
	Stable	Unstable	Subtotal	Stable	Unstable	Subtotal	JVs
Manufacturing — Beamish	5(42%)	7(58%)	12(100%)	31(57%)	23(43%)	54(100%)	66
Aluminum industry — Stuckey	12(44%)	15(56%)	27(100%)	23(70%)	10(30%)	33(100%)	60
Total	17(44%)	22(56%)	39(100%)	54(62%)	33(38%)	87(100%)	126

joint venture. The research partially controlled for this by including in the sample only ventures which had been in existence for at least three years. Sufficient data were, however, not available to correlate stability with age any further.

2.4 PERFORMANCE

In Beamish's (1984) sample, MNE managers assessed 61 per cent of their joint ventures as unsatisfactory performers. In itself, this statistic is useful because it provides some perspective on just how pervasive performance problems are with joint ventures in the developing countries. This is contrasted with the much lower 37 per cent level found in developed countries. These differences are summarised in Table 2.2.

Most of the joint ventures in the LDC sample that ceased operations did so because they failed. However, it would be technically incorrect to class all ventures that have ceased operations as unsatisfactory performers. For example, in one case the local government partner bought out the foreign partner's share in a venture after six years because they felt locals were finally capable of running it (which the foreign partner reluctantly agreed was true). Also, some ventures cease operations for reasons unrelated to being a joint venture or as part of an intentional strategy. These are all exceptions, however.

Many joint ventures involve more than two partners. For example, in Reynolds' (1979) sample of 53 Indian-American joint ventures, 28 involved more than a single Indian partner, and of the balance, public shareholders were present in 15 other cases.

14

There was no difference in performance between ventures with two, or more than two, partners. Twenty of the 66 joint ventures in Beamish's (1984) sample were located in the Caribbean. The performance rates in Caribbean countries and other LDCs were comparable (Table 2.4).

Table 2.4: Venture location — performance relationship

	Satisfactory performance	Unsatisfactory performance	Total	% of total unsatisfactory
JVs in Caribbean countries	7	13	20	65
JVs in other LDCs	19	27	46	58
Total	26	40	66	61

2.5 FREQUENCY OF GOVERNMENT PARTNERS

Few of the studies of joint ventures in developed countries made mention of significant involvement of government partners. However, where the scale of investment was particularly high, or the business lay in an industrial sector important to the local economy, the use of government partners was higher. For example, in Stuckey's (1983) study of joint ventures in the aluminium industry, there was government involvement in 45 per cent of cases.

In Beamish's (1984) LDC sample, 23 of the 66 ventures involved the foreign private firm having either government partners, public shareholders, or other foreign partners. In addition, in only two of the 23 cases was the foreign partner satisfied with the joint venture's performance; none of the twelve ventures with government partners was deemed satisfactory. Given higher frequency of joint venture formation between foreign, private and local government firms in LDCs, these performance results are particularly striking. Yet these observations are consistent with those of other joint-venture research. In an LDC-based sample, Raveed and Renforth (1983) found that MNE executives favour forming joint ventures with local, private firms over all other forms of foreign equity-investment — including both wholly-owned subsidiaries and the other joint-venture forms.

Foreign private firms that had a local private partner were

15

satisfied with performance much more often than with other types of partners (although overall satisfaction was still lower than in samples from developed countries). These performance observations provide support for the view that for MNEs to be successful they require partners with knowledge of the local economy, politics and customs.

2.6 OWNERSHIP

The use of equal ownership was advocated by Killing (1983) in developed-country ventures. However, one writer on joint ventures in developing countries felt that, 'What should be ruled out is a 50-50 shareholding (since) this will invariably lead to a deadlock in corporate decision-making.'[1]

In the LDC samples of both Beamish (1984) and Reynolds (1979), for the majority (70 per cent) of cases the foreign firm was in a minority equity position with only a small proportion (10 to 20 per cent) of the JVs being 50-50 membership. This contrasts sharply with developed-country samples, where half had 50-50 ownership (Table 2.5).

Table 2.5: Joint venture ownership in developed and developing countries

		Frequency of equal-equity (50-50) ventures %	Frequency of majority or minority-equity ventures %
Developed country samples	Mergers & Acquisitions (153)	43	57
	Killing (40)	50	50
	Geringer (86)	70	30
Developing countries	Mergers & Acquisitions (47)	20	80
	Beamish (66)	10	90
	Reynolds (51)	20	80

In an effort to verify the representativeness of the ownership levels found in the developed-country sample and the LDC samples, an examination was made of the ownership percentages noted in the Joint Venture Rosters of the management journal, *Mergers and Acquisitions* over the period 1972–7. Of the approximately 1,000 joint ventures described, ownership detail was provided on 200 cases. Of the 153 JVs which took place between two firms in developed countries, 43 per cent were equally owned. This is comparable to other developed-country samples, where 50 per cent were equally owned. In contrast, 80 per cent of the 47 ventures from *Mergers and Acquisitions* (1972–7) that took place between firms in developed and developing countries were majority- or minority-owned. A similar level was found in this LDC sample.

Also, Berg and Friedman (1978) noted that just over 80 per cent of two-partner, US chemical joint ventures formed between 1924 and 1969 had a 50-50 equity split. This again reinforces the high incidence of equal-equity ventures in developed countries, a situation that is in contrast to developing-country ventures.

Multinationals have in many cases succeeded in accommodating LDC aspirations for local dominance or equality in the shareholdings of local joint ventures. The MNEs have been able to accommodate the LDC desires by spreading the ownership of each venture over a wider number of parties. As a result, the MNE's share of the equity might still be equal to or greater than that of the largest other shareholder.

In Beamish's (1984) LDC sample, when the MNE owned less than 50 per cent of the equity, there was a greater likelihood of satisfactory performance. Also, MNEs which were minority or equal partners performed better than those cases where the MNE was the single, largest shareholder. Strong cases were made by the foreign and local partners in support of being both minority and equal-equity partners.

The most common reasons cited for a multinational taking a minority equity position were existing regulations and/or local tax advantages. However, the range of reasons cited was wide. One executive explained his decision to take a minority position by noting that 'with a high level of corruption in the country, it is better not to be high profile'. A joint venture general manager noted that 'those businesses in which the parent company holds less than 50 per cent of the equity appear in the overall financial statements simply as an investment. This means parent company involvement can be much lower.' Perhaps the most telling reason given for 50-50 equity arrangements was, as one executive noted, that 'then you can't afford to quarrel'.

2.7 OWNERSHIP-CONTROL RELATIONSHIP

Numerous researchers have correctly pointed out that there is no necessary correlation between ownership and control. While there is no necessary correlation, in practice a correlation has often existed, particularly in developed countries. There were strong links in Killing's (1983) sample of joint ventures in developed countries between ownership and control. Seventy per cent of his dominant-management control ventures (those operated like wholly-owned subsidiaries) were majority-owned. Conversely, 76 per cent of the shared-management control ventures in his sample were equally owned by the partners. In the developed-country sample of joint ventures, when the MNE was the minority partner its role was often a silent one. This did not hold true in LDCs.

Researchers of joint ventures in developing countries have previously pointed out that local joint-venture partners are rarely passive shareholders. In Stopford and Wells' (1972) survey, 88 per cent of MNE respondents indicated that the local partner typically had at least some voice in management. In Schaan's (1983) sample of joint ventures in Mexico, all would be classed as having shared control. In Beamish's (1984) research, no correlation could be claimed between ownership and control because the MNE had majority ownership in only 21 per cent of cases.

2.8 CONTROL-PERFORMANCE RELATIONSHIP

In his study of joint ventures in developed countries, Killing (1983) defined control in terms of the decision-making role of joint-venture management, that is, whether an active or passive role. Here control was measured by administering a questionnaire in which managers were asked to assess the 'jointness' of decision-making regarding nine decisions (product pricing, product design, production scheduling, production process, quality standards, replacing a functional manager, budget sales target, budget cost targets, and budget capital expenditures). To assess the 'jointness' of decision-making, six categories of decisions were considered (made by joint-venture executives alone, made by joint-venture executives with input from local parent, made by joint-venture executives with input from foreign parent, made by local parent alone, made by foreign parent alone, made jointly by parents). Then, depending on the response, ventures were classified as dominant, shared or independently controlled. The performance of dominant-parent ventures — those in which one parent plays a strong decision-making role and the other partner a minor one — was considered to be higher than shared management ventures. Table 2.6 correlates joint-venture performance with the aggregate measure of control for Killing's sample.

Table 2.6: Performance — aggregate control in Killing's developed-country sample

	Dominant control	Shared control
Unsatisfactory performance	3	11
Satisfactory performance	10	9

Because two major detriments to joint-venture performance — use of functional executives from the passive parent, and a major role played by the board of directors — have been removed in dominant-parent ventures, Killing feels they are easier to manage than shared-management ventures, hence, better performance. He adds that dominant-parent ventures are managed much like wholly-owned subsidiaries: *all* operating and strategic decisions are made by the dominant parent. In dominant-parent ventures, all functional managers will come from, or be selected by, the dominant parent. They and the joint-venture general manager will be evaluated on the same basis as plant managers for a wholly-owned subsidiary. In addition, the joint venture will be integrated into the dominant parent's management system. Finally, the board of directors will play a largely ceremonial role.

An important variation on the use of shared control is the notion of split control. As Cantwell and Dunning (1984) note, it is possible to obtain the benefits of each partner's expertise by dividing or splitting decision-making. Thus while neither partner has dominant control, nor is every decision jointly made. Geringer (1986) provides empirical support for this view.

The third type of venture in this typology (besides dominant and shared) was independent, in which the joint-venture management team was highly autonomous — receiving little direction from either parent. All of the joint ventures in the Beamish (1984) sample were managed by people supplied by one of the partners, in contrast to the 16 per cent that were independently managed in Killing's (1983) developed-country sample. Not surprisingly, autonomously managed ventures had the highest performance level of all, since to a certain extent they were independent because of their success.

A second study considering the link between management control and performance, was Schaan's (1983). This study examined parent control in terms of mechanisms used to influence specific activities or decisions. This differed from Killing's work, which focused on the amount of overall control and who did the controlling. Schaan's in-depth study of ten joint ventures in Mexico concluded that parent companies were able to turn joint ventures around by creating a fit between their criteria of joint venture success, the activities or decisions they controlled and the mechanisms they used to exercise control.

A third study that considered the link between management control and performance was Janger's (1980). This American Conference Board report gathered data on the organisation of international joint ventures from 168 joint ventures in both developed and developing countries. Using a management control typology roughly comparable to Killing's, the report concluded that the survey and interviews do not identify either dominant or shared ventures as being more successful than the others.

Tomlinson (1970), in his examination of the joint-venture process in international business, also looked at the control-performance link. In this study of 71 joint ventures in two developing countries, he examined the argument that a greater level of foreign control should lead to greater profitability. Tomlinson found that 'higher levels of return were obtained from joint-venture investments by UK firms with a more relaxed attitude towards control. This casts some doubt upon the theory that control is necessary in order to improve the operational effectiveness of a joint venture' (p. 147). Tomlinson feels the

MNE should not insist on dominant control over the major managerial decisions in the joint venture. He suggests that the sharing of responsibility with local associates will lead to a greater contribution from them and in turn a greater return on investment. What the literature seems to indicate is a different emphasis — in fact a weakening of the link — between dominant management control and good performance when study focus shifts from the developed countries to the less developed countries.

Data were collected on control in joint ventures in developing countries and compared with observations from samples in developed countries. To increase the comparability of results, the measure of control used by Killing in developed countries was used in a sub-sample of Beamish's (1984) sample. In the LDC sample however, consideration was given within the dominant-control category as to whether this control was from the foreign or local partner. In the LDC sample, a strong correlation was observed between unsatisfactory performance and dominant foreign control. In only a small minority of cases however was unsatisfactory performance associated with local partner involvement in decision-making control.

Further reinforcement for the importance of shared decision-making control in LDCs was observed when each individual decision was related to control. For example, control was always shared for the generally conceded important decision of capital expenditures, while one of the partners always had dominant control over the less-important decision regarding production scheduling.

2.9 CONCLUSION

Table 2.7 summarises the eight differences noted in joint venture characteristics between developed and developing countries. Performance problems whether measured in terms of stability or by managerial assessment — were observed to be higher in LDCs. This held true even when the effect of poor performing business-government ventures in LDCs was taken into consideration.

The major implication of these findings for managers is to suggest that their approach to joint ventures in developed and developing countries should differ. For example, they can now recognise that their typical pattern of involvement with joint ventures (i.e. equal equity, dominant control) is neither common nor likely desirable in LDCs.

By knowing before the original investment is made that the management of joint ventures may be affected by the different environments, managers can assess better whether they should enter a joint venture in an LDC, and improve their understanding as to why their existing ventures perform the way they do.

Table 2.7: Summary of differences of joint-venture characteristics

	Developed country	Developing country
Major reason for creating venture	Skill required (64%)	Government suasion (57%)
Instability rate	30%	45%
MNE managerial assessment of dissatisfaction with performance	37%	61%
Frequency of association with government partners	Low	Moderate
Most common level of ownership for MNE	Equal	Minority
Ownership-control relationship	Direct (dominant control with majority ownership; shared control with equal ownership)	Difficult to discern because most MNEs have a minority ownership position.
Control-performance relationship in successful JVs	Dominant control	Shared or split control
Number of autonomously managed ventures	Small (16%)	Negligible (0%)

NOTES

*An earlier version of this chapter appeared in *The Columbia Journal of World Business* and is reproduced with permission.

1. Canadian Consulate-General in Brazil (1981), *Joint business ventures in Brazil: a Canadian perspective*, Ottawa: Department of Industry, Trade and Commerce, Government of Canada, April, p. 7.

3

Partner Selection and Performance*

3.1 INTRODUCTION

The largest part of this research investigates the effect on joint-venture performance of two variables to which other researchers had paid limited attention — need and commitment. Following a series of pilot-survey interviews involving 32 joint ventures in LDCs, the potential impact of these variables upon performance emerges. It is hypothesised that greater need and commitment between partners result in more satisfactory performance. Emphasis on ensuring the long-term viability of the venture underlies the discussion of success in this research. Joint-venture performance is defined according to whether there is mutual agreement between the partners regarding their overall satisfaction.

This chapter focuses on one of these variables — partner need. Partner need is assessed over a span of time in terms of the relative importance of each partner's contribution to the joint venture in a number of aspects such as capital, knowledge and staff.

Of the 66 joint ventures in the study, the most in-depth study and analysis took place on twelve ventures. Overall, seven of these twelve ventures were considered satisfactory performers and the remainder, unsatisfactory. Of the 18 questionnaires administered to parent-company executives and general managers involved in the core ventures, twelve were multi-national executives, three were MNE-supplied general managers, and three were local partners who also acted as general managers.

3.2 PARTNER NEED: LITERATURE AND MEASURES

The pilot-survey observations indicated that what distinguished a successful from an unsuccessful joint venture was not primarily an issue of control, as the literature had suggested. When the problems and characteristics of the highest- and lowest-performing ventures in the pilot survey were compared, a clear pattern with respect to joint-venture performance resulted. Most problems could be viewed in terms of whether there existed mutual long-term need between the partners and commitment of the partners to the use of joint ventures. This section reviews the existing literature on partner need and outlines the measures subsequently used to assess them in the core ventures.

Literature on partner need in joint ventures

Many writers consider mutual long-term need between partners an important issue in assessing a venture's potential. While partner need has seldom received explicit attention, nearly all researchers into joint ventures have included reference to it in their analyses. The most common instances are discussions regarding the long-term need for a partner or the need for one potential partner as opposed to another. This theme can be traced from the early work of Friedmann and Beguin (1971) which stressed the difficulty of choosing a partner when the political, economic and social environment was rapidly changing. Franko (1972), Robock and Simmonds (1973), and Killing (1983) all observed a similar pattern in joint ventures. They noticed that joint ventures were formed as a result of uncertainty concerning a new market; apparent learning about the market followed; then, need for a partner waned. The Canadian Consulate-General's Report (1981) on the establishing of joint ventures in Brazil stressed the value of finding a partner with the same short-term and long-term goals so that the local partner will continue to have a need for the foreign company.

Because any firm that does not *need* a partner will not form a joint venture, it is surprising to find only two pieces of research with detailed lists of partner needs. These two sources are Stopford and Wells (1972) and Raveed and Renforth (1983). Stopford and Wells developed the most complete list of partner needs available at the time, and they were the first researchers to make an attempt to measure the magnitude of different partner needs. They started with a list of nine items, which their questionnaire respondents extended to eleven. Thus, the work of Stopford and Wells served as a starting point for the list of needs measured in this research and was expanded to make it more complete.

Need measurement will be explained in the section following. At this time, note that a more comprehensive list of potential partner needs was developed and then measured from several different perspectives. Because this list was derived from the literature, the list is discussed before need measurement is explained.

Typology of need

There are a large number of potential partner needs, and these can be classified in various ways. In this research, partner needs were divided into five groups (items readily capitalised, human-resource needs, market-access needs, government/political needs, and knowledge needs) of three (or in one case, four) items each. The items making up each of the five groups are discussed in turn.

(i) Items readily capitalised. Virtually all research (including this) includes 'capital' itself on the list of partner needs. In fact, to Roulac (1980) capital was one of the only two reasons for which partners are needed (the other was expertise). The second reason included for needing a partner was to ensure a raw material supply. A third item was technology or equipment. Many firms in developed countries look for local partners as a means of spreading the introduction of their technology to as many markets as possible.

(ii) Human-resource needs. Stopford and Wells (1972) included general managers, marketing personnel, and experienced production, R&D, or technical personnel. However, in this research 'general managers' represented one category, while all 'functional managers' make up the second. The third human-resource need added here was access to a low-cost labour force. Local partners may be more readily able to provide such a labour force than the multinational could if operating a wholly-owned subsidiary.

25

(iii) Market-access needs. Stopford and Wells included three items here. The first — better access to the foreign local market for goods produced outside of it — was modified to include the possibility of the local partner needing a foreign partner to gain better access to foreign markets for goods produced locally. Local partners may want a foreign partner for access to export markets, as Janger (1980) points out. Stopford and Wells' second item — better local access than would have been possible with a wholly-owned subsidiary — was modified to include better access through joint ventures to any markets, again reflecting the LDC partners' perspective. Part of this second item includes a partner need mentioned by Killing (1978): channels of distribution. The third, from Stopford and Wells — speed of entry into the local market — was modified to 'speed of entry into either the local or foreign market'.

(iv) Government/political needs. These were the items that respondents added to Stopford and Wells' initial nine-point list. Both of the items — to meet government requirements for local ownership and to gain political advantage — were retained as separate measures in this research. As part of 'need to meet government requirements', 'need to meet government import substitution policy' as suggested by Hills (1978) was included.

The third partner-need item included in this section was 'to satisfy forecast government requirements for local ownership'. Poynter's (1982) research has highlighted the domestication or localisation tendencies of many LDC governments. This is an important consideration, so the need to forecast changes was added as a separate category. Using joint ventures as a means of reducing the political risk of intervention represents a logical decision for many companies operating in strategic sectors of a local economy. Those ventures operating in strategic sectors are identified in the research. The fourth partner-need item in this section was local political advantages, which includes better political access. Thus, the three items of government/political need differ in concerns for existing requirements, possible requirements and potential advantages.

(v) Knowledge needs. The only item from Stopford and Wells included in this category — general knowledge of the local economy, politics and customs — was retained in this research. Newbould et al (1978) helped to clarify what general knowledge

encompasses by describing it as 'knowledge concerning operating conditions, labour laws, factory regulations, customers,
and marketing methods'. The second item, general knowledge
of the foreign economy, politics and customs, was included to
reflect the perspective of LDC partners. The final item was
knowledge of current business practices, which represented the
other side of the foreign partners' need for an inexpensive
labour force. In this case primary beneficiaries are local
nationals: they acquire knowledge of it, and experience with,
current business practices in exchange for labour.

The focus of the study by Raveed and Renforth (1983) was on
how well state enterprise-multinational corporation joint
ventures met both partners' needs. They surveyed multinational
executives and local elites (neither of which was necessarily
involved in joint ventures) in Costa Rica concerning attitudes
towards a number of forms of foreign-equity investment. In
addition to favouring joint ventures with local private firms over
all other forms, MNE executives felt that the two most important of the foreign-firm objectives were to obtain country-related
knowledge and local management. Joint-venture managers in
the work of Stopford and Wells had similarly ranked these
among the most important local-partner contributions.

Measuring need

The emphasis in this research was on determining level, type and
change (if any) of partner need — both within and between each
parent company. Albeit on a smaller sample, this research
extended the measurement of need in the following ways:

a) Beyond a single point in time (entry), to include the present
   and a forecast of three years hence;
b) Beyond a single perspective (the multinationals'), to
   include the local partner and joint venture general
   manager;
c) To joint ventures specific to developing countries; and
d) To include a larger number of potential partner needs.

**3.3 PARTNER NEED: ANALYSIS AND RELATIONSHIP TO
PERFORMANCE**

Firms establishing joint ventures typically need partners for a

27

variety of potential contributions. Based on a statistical analysis of the questionnaire responses, supplemented by the interview comments of MNE executives, a relatively clear picture emerged with respect to the contributions important to each partner, the contributions characteristically important in the high- and low-performing ventures, and those contributions of long-term, short-term and of little importance.

Part of the questionnaire focused on the interviewee's assessment of the importance of his partner's contribution to the venture of 16 different items. The relative importance of each item was measured at three times: at entry, the present, and three years hence.

Needs of long-term importance were defined as those which were steadily important or increasingly important, at a minimum significance level of .05 or lower. Needs of short-term importance were those which were important, but decreasingly so. Needs were unimportant if they were steadily unimportant at a statistical significance level of .05 or lower. Significance levels up to .20 are reported however, because of the small sample constraint, because values to this level are often included with the Kolmogorov-Smirnov test, and because they are useful in suggesting direction. The original pilot survey focus on long-term rather than short-term partner need was extended to include a more absolute view of partner need since this more accurately reflects the situation in which one partner has *no* need for a particular partner contribution.

When the words important/unimportant are used, this is a reference to the five-point scale used in the questionnaire. In any case where a contribution is described as important or unimportant, this means at a statistical significance level of .05 or lower. Those items with significance levels of .20 or lower can be found in Table 3.1. There were six items important to the executives in the high-performing ventures at .20 significance or lower — four of which were significant at 0.05 or lower. The executives from the low-performing ventures felt that the partner made important contributions (both at .05 significance or lower) in only two areas.

Partner contributions

Each of the 16 partner contributions which formed this part of the questionnaire was hypothesised as important either by a previous researcher or by an executive interviewed during the pilot survey. Each contribution and its relationship to performance is examined in terms of:

a) Degree of importance (i.e. important, neutral, unimportant);
b) Changes in importance (i.e. increasing, decreasing, steady, and — as occurred only with the unimportant partner contributions — dual directional variation over time); and
c) The various perspectives (i.e. MNE executives, local partner/general manager). There were also completed questionnaires from three MNE-supplied general managers; however their responses tended to be quite similar to those of their foreign parents. Therefore, only major differences are noted. Although these sample sizes are small, the Kolmogorov-Smirnov test was specifically chosen to accommodate this fact.

Each of the 16 partner contributions is examined. The results are summarised from the various perspectives in terms of degree of importance and changes in importance in Table 3.1. It bears mention that most of the MNE executives in the ventures classed as low performers were satisfied with their venture's performance. It is unlikely that multinational executives downplayed their partner's contribution because they were dissatisfied with the venture's performance. Consequently, concerns regarding causality can be alleviated.

1) Faster entry into local market. The twelve multinational executives as a group did not feel that this was an important contribution of their local partner. There was no difference in the response rates from executives in the high- and low-performing ventures. As expected, in half the cases the relative importance of this partner contribution to the multinational declined over time. What was initially surprising was that this item retained *any* importance to MNEs over time. The explanation: some respondents felt that their partners continued to contribute faster entry for new products introduced to the local market after start-up. In several cases, respondents also interpreted 'faster entry into market' to include 'faster later entry through exports to other regional markets'. Not surprisingly, the local

29

Table 3.1: Summary of partner contributions

	To MNEs in high-performing JVs[4]	To MNEs in low-performing JVs[4]	To local general managers[4]
Needs of long-term importance[1]	5) Local business knowledge 8) General managers 10) Knowledge of local economy, politics and customs 13) Functional managers		15) Better export opportunities
Needs of short-term importance[2]	2) Local political advantages 7) Avoid political intervention	7) Avoid political intervention 11) Meet existing government ownership requirements	4) Raw material supply 12) Technology or equipment
Unimportant needs[3]	3) Inexpensive labour 4) Raw material supply 12) Technology or equipment	3) Inexpensive labour 4) Raw material supply 12) Technology or equipment 13) Functional managers 14) Access to local market 15) Better export opportunities	1) Speed of entry 2) Local political advantages 3) Inexpensive labour 10) Knowledge of local economy, politics and customs

Notes:
1. Steadily or increasingly important over time.
2. Decreasingly important over time.
3. Unimportant.
4. Numbers refer to questionnaire order.

shareholders deemed their foreign partner's contribution of faster entry into the local market as unimportant.

2) Local political advantages. The executives in the high-performing ventures felt their local partner's contribution of local political advantages tended (.10 significance versus the required .05 level) to be important. However, the multinational executives felt that their partner's contribution did decline slightly with time. Whether this was due to an overall decline in the perceived importance of local political advantages or, as one foreign executive noted, 'because we have personally become more involved politically as our stake in the country has increased' is not clear. By 'involved politically' the executive meant that he had developed closer social, and to a lesser extent working, ties to members of the ruling political party.

Having a politically well-connected partner was certainly no guarantee of joint-venture success. Several of the politically most powerful local partners were associated with two of the low-performing joint ventures. In other cases, local partners were clearly able to provide local political advantages. Again, not surprisingly, the local shareholders deemed their foreign partner's contribution of local political advantages unimportant.

3) Inexpensive labour. All respondents unanimously rated their partners' contribution of an inexpensive labour supply as unimportant (.01 significance level). There was total agreement that any potentially beneficial effect of lower wage rates was negated by the impact of overemployment, generally poorer employee training and working conditions, looser controls, a different work ethic, the use of less productive older machinery, and utility service interruptions.

4) Raw material supply. The multinational executives from both the high- and low-performing ventures deemed unimportant their partners' contribution of raw material supply (.01 significance). Conversely, this was one of only three areas in which the local shareholders felt that foreign partners made an important contribution (.05 significance), although this was true only at the time of entry.

There was a slight but distinctive trend for the multinational executives to look increasingly to their local partners for a raw

31

material contribution, and for the local partners increasingly to downplay the importance of the foreign partners' contribution. One executive suggested that this trend was a natural consequence of the national development over the years of the local country. As the country developed, it had become increasingly possible to acquire raw materials locally. It remained common practice in most joint ventures, however, for the foreign partners to supply raw materials.

5) Knowledge of current business practices. This item was originally designed to examine whether local partners perceived any contribution from their partners in knowledge of current, foreign business practices. There was no clear pattern of responses from the local shareholders for this item. The multinational executives in turn interpreted this question to mean 'knowledge of current *local* business practices'. Therefore, their responses were similar to the more inclusive item ten, 'general knowledge of the local economy, politics, and customs'. The multinational executives in the high-performing ventures rated their partners' contribution of 'knowledge of current local business practices' as important (.05 significance) at both the present and for the future. The responses of the multinational executives from the low-performing ventures, however, were uniformly distributed.

For many of the items examined, the responses of the foreign-supplied general manager and the foreign parent were quite similar. For this particular item, however, the general managers always rated the local partners' contribution of 'knowledge of current local business practices' lower than had their foreign parent companies. If we could assume that general managers normally spend more time with the local partners than the foreign parents do, then it would be possible to suggest that multinationals were overestimating their partners' potential contribution. However, this was not the case. Two of the three ventures in which foreign-supplied GMs were interviewed were low performers. Hence, a more reasonable interpretation is that the general managers might do well to solicit the local partners' contribution of 'knowledge of current local business practices' more often. In only the high-performing venture was the general manager a national of the local country. Consequently, we would expect that there would legitimately be a lower need for the partners' contribution in this area.

6) Better access to markets than a wholly-owned subsidiary would provide. The major reason for establishing a joint venture (rather than a wholly-owned subsidiary) in the developing countries was government suasion or regulations (chapter 2). Consequently, one might expect multinational executives to evaluate the potential contributions of 'better access' as unimportant because it is not necessarily related to government influence. In fact, there was no clear pattern of response from the multinationals. Some firms perceived the existence of government suasion, while others in the same industry sector and country did not. Since the multinationals did not feel that this contribution was unimportant, this suggests that the decision to form a joint venture rather than a wholly-owned subsidiary is based on more than just the local government's desires.

7) Satisfy expected government requirements for local ownership/avoid political intervention. At entry into the joint venture, executives from both the high- and low-performing ventures rated this item as an important contribution of their local partners. This contribution was particularly relevant to the executives from the low-performing ventures (.05 significance, versus .20 significance with high-performers); in fact, it was one of only two items in which they felt the local partner made an important contribution. What is significant about this is that it is the type of contribution in which virtually any partner will suffice. Unlike more specific partner contributions such as supplying the general manager, the partner is chosen here primarily because, as a national of the country, he satisfies the government's local-ownership requirements.

This result is consistent with the response received to the question, 'Did you need a partner with specific qualifications?' This open-ended question had been asked of the respondents before they completed the partner-need questionnaire. In eight of the twelve ventures, there was agreement that a partner with specific qualifications was required. Significance lay in that three of the four responses which indicated that a specific partner was not required were from poorly-performing ventures.

The MNE expectations of ownership requirements and/or political intervention generally declined with time. Four of the five firms showing a decline were located in the main Caribbean country where the core ventures were located. This decline can reasonably be attributed to a change in local government. It was also interesting to observe how executives in the same industry and same country differed widely in their expectations of government ownership requirements or political intervention. In several cases, the inability of executives to assess accurately political risk caused multinationals to form a joint venture when they did not want to — but thought they had no choice.

8) General managers. Of all the items in the need questionnaire, this exhibited the greatest difference in response from the MNE executives of high-performing as contrasted with low-performing ventures. At all three points in time, the multinational executives from the high-performing ventures deemed important their partners' contribution of general managers (.05 significance). In contrast, multinational executives from the low-performing ventures considered their partners' contribution in this area unimportant (.05 significance).

Given the large expense of maintaining expatriate managers in foreign countries, many multinationals try to minimise the use of foreign managers. Several of the multinationals noted, however, that they liked to have at least one of their own people in the joint venture to 'look after their interests'. Yet, in all three ventures where the local partner acted as general manager, the venture was a high performer. As one executive noted, 'a "good" national knows how to move around the local government bureaucracy'. Interestingly, the assessment of the importance of this item from executives in three of the five low-performing ventures did increase over time.

9) Capital. With respect to either partner's contribution of capital, there was no clear pattern (a) between foreign and local partners; (b) between high and low performers; or (c) in change over time.

10) General knowledge of the local economy, politics and culture. The multinational executives from the high-performing ventures rated this as the most important contribution (.05 significance) of their local partners at all three points in time. No such relationship was found in the responses from the low-performing ventures. Stopford and Wells had found this the most important partner contribution at the time of entry into the joint venture. However, they did not obtain a measure of the partners' contribution at the present time or three years hence, nor examine the relationship between each contribution and performance.

In many cases, this partner contribution of general knowledge took place on a regular basis. In other cases, the partner's contribution was more subtle. One multinational executive noted that, 'We need our partner in the same way that a child playing in a park still likes to have his parent around if he gets into trouble. It's not that the child is dependent on the parent, but more a function of being reassured that he's there if needed.'

The relative importance of the local partner's contribution of this general knowledge did exhibit a very slight decline with time in four of the twelve ventures. The implication here is that the multinationals can ultimately learn for themselves about the local economy, politics and culture. However, as one manager noted, 'In [this LDC], you have to understand the atmosphere more than anything — and that takes time.' Another executive expressed the same point this way: 'One has a strong need for the partners' knowledge of the local market in the developing countries since it would take us 20-or-so years to learn how to manage in it. The reason is that the locals have the mentality or mental outlook as to what is acceptable or unacceptable in the country.'

11) Meet existing government requirements for local ownership or import substitution. At the time of entry into the joint ventures, the multinational executives from low-performing ventures felt that this was an important contribution (.05 significance) of their local partner. They rated its importance almost identical to the similar seventh item — Satisfy Expected Government Requirements for Local Ownership/Avoid Political Intervention. These two items were the only ones in which the local partners in low-performing ventures were regarded as making an important contribution. As noted earlier, it is the type of partner contribution for which nearly any partner would suffice. The responses in the high-performing ventures were uniformly distributed.

12) Technology or equipment. At all points in time, the executives in both the high- and low-performing ventures felt that this was an unimportant contribution (.01 significance) of their local partner. Conversely, and as expected, the local shareholders considered this to be one of the three areas in which the

Table 3.2: Summary of partner-need questionnaire responses

Abbreviated statement from questionnaire[1]	Point in time of measure	Aggregate of 12 MNE executives	The MNE executives in 7 high-performing ventures	The MNE executives in 5 low-performing ventures	The 3 equity-holding general managers
1) Faster entry	Entry	.20	—	—	—
	Present	—	—	—	(.05)[2]
	Future	—	—	—	(.05)
2) Local political advantages	Entry	.10	.10	—	—
	Present	.15	—	—	(.05)
	Future	—	—	—	—
3) Inexpensive labour	Entry	(.01)[2]	(.01)[2]	(.01)[2]	(.05)
	Present	(.01)	(.01)	(.01)	(.05)
	Future	(.01)	(.01)	(.01)	(.15)
4) Raw material supply	Entry	(.01)	(.01)	(.05)	.05
	Present	(.01)	(.05)	—	—
	Future	(.01)	(.05)	(.05)	—
5) Local business knowledge	Entry	—	—	—	—
	Present	.05	.01	—	—
	Future	—	.05	—	—
6) Better market access	Entry	—	—	—	—
	Present	—	—	—	—
	Future	—	—	—	—
7) Satisfy expected government requirements/ avoid political intervention	Entry	.15	.20	.05	—
	Present	—	—	—	—
	Future	—	—	—	—
8) General managers	Entry	—	.05	(.05)	—
	Present	—	.01	—	—
	Future	—	.05	—	—
9) Capital	Entry	—	—	—	—
	Present	—	—	—	—
	Future	—	—	—	—
10) Knowledge of local economy, politics and culture	Entry	.01	.01	—	—
	Present	.05	.05	—	(.05)
	Future	—	.05	—	(.15)

Table 3.2: — *continued*

Abbreviated statement from questionnaire[1]	Point in time of measure	Aggregate of 12 MNE executives	The MNE executives in 7 high-performing ventures	The MNE executives in 5 low-performing ventures	The 3 equity-holding general managers
11) Meeting existing government requirements	Entry	.05	—	.05	—
	Present	—	—	—	—
	Future	—	—	—	—
12) Technology or equipment	Entry	(.01)	(.01)	(.01)	.05
	Present	(.01)	(.01)	(.01)	—
	Future	(.01)	(.01)	(.01)	—
13) Functional managers	Entry	—	—	(.05)	—
	Present	—	—	—	—
	Future	—	.05	(.05)	—
14) Access to local market	Entry	.20	—	—	—
	Present	—	—	—	(.05)
	Future	—	—	—	(.05)
15) Better export opportunities	Entry	—	—	(.05)	—
	Present	—	—	(.05)	—
	Future	—	—	(.05)	.05
16) Knowledge of foreign economy, politics and culture	Entry	—	—	—	—
	Present	—	—	—	—
	Future	—	—	—	—

Notes:
1. Kolmogorov-Smirnov One-Sample Test used to derive significance levels.
2. Bracketed numeric values indicate that this statement is considered an unimportant contribution of the partner; unbracketed values indicate the statement is considered an important contribution.
3. Given the small sample sizes in some cases, it is difficult to attain statistically significant findings of .05 or lower.

foreign partners made an important contribution. These results are consistent with the traditional thinking on the role of technology in LDCs. The successful transfer of technology or equipment from the foreign to the local country did not, however, guarantee success for the joint venture. While some ventures encountered difficulties as a result of technology or equipment, most MNEs were able to transfer successfully both physical goods and process to a local country. Especially in the core ventures, there was a recognition that more was involved than the physical transfer of equipment and operating manuals. In most cases, sufficient time was allocated to permit the local partner to understand technological processes being transferred.

13) Functional managers (marketing, production, financial, etc.). At both the time of entry into the joint venture and for the future, the multinational executives from low-performing ventures felt that their local partners' contribution of functional managers was unimportant (.05 significance). However, the multinational executives from the high-performing ventures felt that their partners' contribution of functional managers would be important (.05 significance) in the future. These results are both similar to the multinational executives' assessment of their local partners' contribution of General Managers.

14) Better access to the local market for goods produced outside it. Multinational executives from low-performing ventures felt that their local partners' contribution of better access to the local market for goods produced outside it was unimportant at both the present and for the future (.05 significance). Responses of multinational executives from the high-performing ventures were uniformly distributed.

15) Better export opportunities. As with the previous item, multinational executives from the low-performing ventures felt that their partners' contribution of better export opportunities was unimportant (.05 significance). The responses of the multinational executives from the high-performing ventures were uniformly distributed. This was, however, the third area in which the local shareholders looked to their foreign partners for an important contribution, in this case expecting the contribution to become increasingly important (.05 significance) in the future.

16) General knowledge of the foreign economy, politics and culture. The responses to this question were uniformly distributed for both groups of multinational respondents. The question had, however, been primarily designed for the local partners. Two of the three local shareholders did feel that their foreign partner made a contribution in this regard. This was consistent with their looking to the multinationals for better export opportunities. The problem which many local partners faced, however, was that multinationals had already staked out the countries to which each subsidiary or joint venture was allowed to export.

17) Other. There were several items not included on the list provided, to which multinational executives felt their local partners made important contributions. These were: (a) help on board decisions; (b) knowledge of local financing; and (c) as a guide to 'figures of importance' on the local scene.

3.4 TIME DIMENSION OF PARTNER NEED

An analysis was conducted using the Kolmogorov-Smirnov One-Sample Test to determine which partner needs changed over time. Partner contributions which were considered unimportant tended to remain unimportant, while contributions considered important tended to vary in importance over time.

Four of the ten total contributions rated as unimportant by the high-performing MNEs, low-performing MNEs and local general managers/partners, steadily remained unimportant with time. To be defined as steadily unimportant, i.e. .05 significance in any period, significance levels could not change by more than .05 across the three periods. For example, both the high- and low-performing MNEs never looked to their local partners for technology or equipment. Yet, the MNE executives from the high-performing ventures certainly seemed much clearer with regard to which partner contributions they regarded as unimportant. The fact that MNE partners in low-performing ventures changed their assessments about the contributions their partners could make supports the earlier notion, that for success in LDCs, MNEs have need(s) for their partners which are more concrete and specific than simply to satisfy government regulations.

Only two of the nine partner contributions rated as important remained steadily important. These were the need for knowledge of the local economy, politics and customs and the need for general managers. Both were important to the MNE executives in the high-performing ventures.

PARTNER SELECTION AND PERFORMANCE

Four important partner contributions decreased in importance. The MNE partners in the low-performing ventures assessed the local partners' contributions as being decreasingly important in satisfying expected government requirements and avoiding political intervention. Similarly the local partners assessed their MNE partners' contributions as being decreasingly important for raw material supply, and for technology or equipment.

Three partner contributions increased in importance. Two of these three contributions were important to the MNE executives in the high-performing ventures (local business knowledge, functional managers), while the other was increasingly important to the local partners (better export opportunities).

Given the way that the relative importance of these partner contributions varies, it is valid to view partner need in dynamic terms; there are both long- and short-term needs. In addition, however, it is correct to assess the relative importance of certain needs in absolute terms; certain needs either exist or they do not, and their condition does not generally vary.

3.5 AGGREGATE PARTNER CONTRIBUTIONS

The multinational executives in aggregate felt that speed of entry was an important partner contribution at the time of establishing the joint venture. These same executives agreed that raw material supply, inexpensive labour supply, and technology/equipment were not important partner contributions.

The three local managers, all of whom were partners in high-performing ventures, felt that the foreign multinationals made important contributions in the areas of raw material supply, technology/equipment and export opportunities. They deemed four potential contributions of the multinationals unimportant: speed of entry into the local market, local political advantages, inexpensive labour supply, and general knowledge of the local economy, politics and customs. Not surprisingly, the important needs of one partner are often the unimportant needs of the other, and *vice versa*.

The lack of need for a partner would result in poor performance in a joint venture for a number of potential reasons. For the purpose of analysis, the reasons can be summarised in terms of efficiency and effectiveness. In any business it is inefficient to increase the number of organisational layers through which decisions flow, if there is no benefit to be derived from the increased communication. If a multinational does not look to its local partner for a contribution, it is not likely to receive one. Worse, however, it is unable to treat the business as a wholly-owned subsidiary, since equity holdings are shared with the local partner. This results in an efficiency cost to the MNE without a corresponding benefit.

In addition to the increased communication costs, most joint-venture partners — even if they normally assume a relatively passive role — have the option of becoming more involved in the operation of the business if they so desire. A number of instances were cited during the research interviews in which hitherto silent partners became more involved in the ventures' operations even though their contribution had been unsought. Given that the essence of a joint venture is the jointness of the decision-making, using this organisational form is not an efficient use of resources when a contribution from the partner is not sought.

Finally, other research on joint ventures in LDCs, as well as· this, has noted the importance attached to the local partners' contribution of knowledge of the local economy, politics and customs. In the majority of instances, local businessmen have a much better understanding than foreigners of this important influence on local business success. To form a joint venture in an LDC and not to make use of the important contribution the local partner can make in this regard represents an ineffective use of available resources.

3.6 CONCLUSION

One of the patterns emergent from this research was that MNE executives in high-performing ventures looked to their local partners for greater contributions than did MNE executives in low-performing ventures. As Table 3.1 demonstrates, MNE executives in high-performing ventures considered that their partners made contributions of long-term importance in four unique areas, while MNE executives in the low-performing ventures did not consider any of their partners' contributions of long-term importance. Conversely, MNE executives from the low-performing ventures regarded their partners' contributions as unimportant in seven areas, while MNE executives from the high-performing ventures considered their partners' contributions unimportant only in three areas.

Multinational executives in the high-performing ventures characteristically looked to local partners for contributions in general managers, functional managers, knowledge of current local business practices, and general knowledge of the local economy, politics and customs. These contributions can be collapsed into two general groups: local management and local knowledge. By way of contrast, multinational executives in low-performing ventures characteristically looked to their partners for contributions in (a) being able to satisfy expected government requirements for local ownership or to avoid political intervention; and similarly (b) meeting existing government requirements for local ownership or import substitution.

The differences between the items considered important to each group are quite interesting. Executives in high-performing ventures generally required *specific* partners to attain desired partner contributions, while executives in the low-performing ventures would be theoretically satisfied with *any* partner as long as he was a national of the local country. Given this lack of interest in acquiring specific contributions from their partners, it is not surprising to find executives from low-performing ventures rating five additional potential contributions as unimportant. These were technology or equipment, general managers, functional managers, better access to the local market for goods produced outside it, and better export opportunities. These differences in attitude between the two types of MNE partners can be traced directly to their original approach to joint ventures. While some firms prefer to operate as wholly-owned subsidiaries, others acknowledge the contributions that local partners can make. As this chapter has shown, what you need a partner for, and for how long, will influence the success of the joint venture.

NOTE

*An earlier version of this chapter appeared in *Management International Review* and is reproduced with permission.

4

Commitment*

4.1 INTRODUCTION

The focus of this chapter is on the role of commitment, one of several constructs found (Beamish, 1984) to be relevant to joint venture success. This chapter shows that there are different types and degrees of commitment, and that commitment can be operationalised in such a way as to help to distinguish between satisfactory and unsatisfactory joint venture performance. The emphasis here complements that of the international development agencies by focusing on management issues, not simply on structural concerns.

The commitment measures developed can be used not only by MNEs but by firms in LDCs to assess whether they should enter a particular joint venture. In addition, where an MNE-local partner joint venture already exists the scale items can be used by the local partner to understand better why the venture is performing the way it is and to provide some insight into the likely effect of any management changes to the venture.

4.2 RATIONALE FOR COMMITMENT

There is a negligible level of discussion in international business literature on the subject of commitment. The only works in the international-business joint-venture literature found emphasising the role of commitment were those of Tomlinson and Willie (1982), Schaan (1983) and Geringer (1986). Commitment to a particular venture was one of the variables Tomlinson and

43

Willie used in modelling the joint-venture process in Latin America. Schaan noted the importance of (a) allocating managerial time to develop a relationship with the partner; (b) transferring knowledge and skills that the venture might lack; and (c) trying to build trust. Geringer found it to be the most important partner selection criterion.

Most of the literature on commitment is in the area of organisational behaviour and is concerned with employee commitment to the organisation. These writers focus on such factors as employees' position in the organisation and tenure with the organisation. One of the earliest researchers, Salancik (1977), who provided the means by which commitment was ultimately measured in the research, noted however that there are more ways in which commitment is relevant to organisations than just staying on the job.

The decision to focus on commitment in this research was a result of comments made by multinational executives interviewed during the pilot survey of 34 joint ventures in LDCs. In the pilot survey, nearly all of the problems associated with managing joint ventures in LDCs could be viewed in terms of whether there existed a mutual long-term need between the partners and whether partners were committed to the joint-venture structure in an international context.

4.3 DEFINITION OF COMMITMENT

Commitment was the word which the multinational executives, and other managers subsequently interviewed, used to describe the degree to which they felt bound to a particular behaviour regarding their joint venture. Executives continually used the word commitment in four general ways: to describe relative attitudes towards international business, towards the use of joint ventures, towards particular ventures, and towards particular partners. On the evidence of early interviews, commitment seemed to have both rational and emotional components. Certainly, a significant portion of what executives called commitment was a function of both their past experiences with joint ventures and an analysis of the pros and cons of using the joint-venture form of organisation. A purely rational view, recognising that both resources and information are limited, would lead to analysis based on an understanding of the trade-offs involved. However, the extent to which executives were willing to bind their companies to the use of joint ventures went beyond this purely rational analysis of the appropriateness of using a joint venture.

In many firms, the attitude of the company towards the use of joint ventures had attained the status of a corporate value — 'We favour the use of joint ventures/We oppose the use of joint ventures.' In many companies it was simply corporate policy always to use, or never to use, joint ventures in developing countries. In one extreme case, an American multinational acquired by a Canadian firm was directed either to buy out, or to sell out to, all of its joint-venture partners.

This also worked the other way: in several cases, ventures that no longer fitted within the corporate portfolio were maintained. Among the reasons given: either it was the first venture established by the person who was now the company chairman, or the company chairman had, over the years, become personally friendly with the partner. Whether or not one agrees that sentiment or personal considerations should play any role in the joint-venture process, in reality they do. Given such a situation, joint-venture commitment is defined as the degree to which a firm is bound to a rationally and/or emotionally derived behaviour; and is evidently a multidimensional construct.

Based on the results of the interviews carried out in the pilot survey it became apparent that the behaviours of primary interest were commitment to a course of action (i.e. to international business and the joint-venture structure) and commitment to a particular project (the specific venture and the specific partner). This use of commitment in relation to a course of action and to a particular project is similar in several ways to its use by Ginzberg (1981) with regards to the implementation of management information systems (MISs). More specifically, commitment to international business is comparable to Ginzberg's commitment to any issue or action necessitated by the new system.

A second issue Ginzberg found relevant to eventual MIS success concerns the gaining of commitment to the particular MIS implementation project. Here, the focus was on taking those actions necessary to ensure the quality of the MIS project. This is similar to commitment to the particular joint venture and the particular venture partner, in that both: a) are specific in direction (i.e. to a particular joint venture or particular MIS implementation project); b) require commitment from different groups of people with different orientations (i.e. in Ginzberg's MIS projects it was users and management; in the case of joint ventures it is the foreign and local partners); and c) required commitment at all stages of the process.

In the case of MIS implementations, commitment issues were placed in the context of a seven-stage model of change. Ginzberg believed that those issues recurring during the sequential stages (scouting, entry, diagnosis, planning, action, evaluation, termination) of the Kolb-Frohman model might be critical issues requiring resolution in order to assure implementation success. In the joint-venture case, commitment to the venture is considered necessary at all three stages of the joint-venture process — decision to form a joint venture, partner selection, and an ongoing management.

Based on the results of the pilot survey a preliminary scale measuring commitment was constructed and subsequently modified during the pre-testing phase of the study.

To measure commitment and its relationships to joint venture performance, the general managers of twelve JVs were asked to complete a questionnaire, the purpose of which was to assess how characteristic a total of 16 statements were of the foreign (MNE) parent-company's attitudes and activities *vis-à-vis* joint ventures and/or the particular joint venture. Commitment was conceptualised along two major dimensions: commitment to a course of action (which in turn was subdivided into commitment to international business and commitment to the joint venture structure), and commitment to the particular project (subdivided into commitment to the particular venture and commitment to the particular partner).

The statements designed to measure commitment to international business were related to: attitude towards foreign investment (generally and in LDCs), to willingness to adapt products to the needs of the local market, and to willingness to increase the number of nationals employed. Note, however, that none of these statements necessarily measures commitment exclusively in one area.

The statements designed to measure commitment to the joint-venture structure were concerned with whether the parent company: was willing to form a joint venture when there were no regulations requiring it to do so; was willing to take a minority-equity position; spent a long time weighing the costs and benefits of using joint ventures over other organisational forms; and had contingency plans for providing its joint ventures with increased levels of assistance if necessary.

Statements designed to measure commitment to a particular venture asked whether joint-venture or parent-company concerns came first; whether parent-company management was willing to visit regularly and to offer assistance to the joint venture; whether parent-company management was willing to commit resources (people, time and money) to the venture even when it should technically acquire these things on its own; and whether, when special skills were required by the joint venture, parent-company management first tried to find them in the parent organisation. Regarding whether the concerns of the joint venture or those of either parent company came first, commitment was assumed to be greater when the joint-venture concerns came first. The implicit belief was that the general manager was best qualified to operate the joint venture, in the context of what both partners had agreed was an appropriate direction. Commitment to the particular venture as used in this research is similar to the measure by Tomlinson and Willie where parent firms' commitment represented their readiness to make a continued, long-term commitment of resources such as financing, technical skills, managerial personnel and senior executives' time. Essentially, it indicated a partner's willingness to provide resources and capabilities.

Commitment to a particular partner was assessed in terms of: willingness to consider seriously changing current working procedures and reporting requirements to accommodate the partner; ensuring through regular meetings that each partner knew what to expect from the joint venture; including the partner even in decisions not requiring joint discussion according to the management agreement; and the amount of time spent with the partner, beyond normal hours, working on venture business. Ratings on each statement were over a five-point scale (uncharacteristic, 1; somewhat uncharacteristic, 2; average, 3; somewhat characteristic, 4; characteristic, 5).

The hypothesis governing all statements was that the more characteristic a statement, the greater the level of commitment, and the better the performance of the joint venture.

4.4 RESULTS

Based on their performance the joint ventures in the sample were classified as either high or low performers. For each group, the Kolgomorov-Smirnov One-Sample Test was applied to see whether the distribution of responses to each of the 16 commitment statements could have come from a random distribution. In the case of the seven high-performing ventures the responses to six statements significantly (at .05 or better) differed from a random distribution, with statements being scored heavily towards the 'characteristic' end of the scale. In the case of low-performing ventures, the responses to one of the 16 items significantly differed from random, with the statement scored towards the 'uncharacteristic' end of the scale. These results are summarised in Table 4.1. The scores of the remaining statements of the commitment scale, while not significantly different from a random distribution, were nonetheless in the hypothesised direction.

In order to make an overall assessment of the commitment scale, the ratings of the 16 statements for each JV were added to form a single score on commitment. The internal consistency reliability of the overall scale as measured by the Cronbach alpha coefficient was .79. While we recognise that the current sample size is far too small to assess the reliability of the commitment scale through Cronbach alpha, the coefficient was calculated in order to provide a preliminary assessment of the scale's reliability. Alpha coefficients greater than .70 are considered adequate for exploratory research (Nunnally 1978; Peter 1979), so that the value obtained for the commitment scale is not discouraging.

The one-tailed t-test of the mean overall commitment scores of the high- and low-performing ventures resulted in a t-value of 2.66, which is significant at .017 (with 10 degrees of freedom). The regression of overall commitment scores against the dependent variable, performance, resulted in an adjusted R-square of .44 and an F-value of 8.88 which is significant at .02 level (with 7 and 9 degrees of freedom for the regression and residual mean squares).

These parametric analyses were carried out mainly with a view to providing a 'feel' for the strength of the underlying relationships. Given the sample size and measurement limitations of the data, they should be interpreted with caution.

Table 4.1: Commitment characteristics of MNE partners, by performance

		MNE responses in high-performing ventures (mean) n = 7	MNE responses in low-performing ventures (mean) n = 5
Commitment to international business	Strong parent company emphasis on foreign investment	–	–
	Favours investment in LDCs	–	–
	Willing to adapt products	Characteristic (4.57)	–
	Willing to increase the number of nationals employed	Characteristic* (4.85)	–
Commitment to the joint-venture structure	Willing to form a joint venture when not required by government	–	–
	Willing to take a minority equity position	–	Uncharacteristic (1.8)
	Does cost/benefit of joint-venture organisation form	–	–
	Has contingency plans for assistance	Characteristic (4.43)	
Commitment to the particular joint venture	Interested in venture concerns before those of parent company	–	–
	Willing to visit and offer assistance	Characteristic* (5.00)	–
	Willing to commit resources	–	–
	Looking for special skills first in parent organisation	Characteristic (4.43)	–
Commitment to the particular venture partner	Willing to change procedures for partner	–	–
	Holds regular meetings	Characteristic* (4.57)	–
	Includes partners in additional discussions	–	–
	Spends time beyond normal hours	–	–

Note: When the words characteristic/uncharacteristic are used, this means at a statistical significance level of .05 or better; the asterisk denotes that the statement is also characteristic of the twelve MNE respondents in aggregate.

Table 4.2: Summary of commitment questionnaire responses

Abbreviated statement from questionnaire[1]	Aggregate of 12 MNE executives	The MNE executives in 7 high-performing ventures	The MNE executive in 5 low-performing ventures	Aggregate of (5)6 general managers	The (2)3 equity-holding general managers	The 3 non-equity holding general managers
1) Foreign investment	.20	—	—	—	—	—
2) LDC foreign investment	—	—	—	—	—	—
3) Adapt products	.10	.05	—	—	—	—
4) Nationals employed	.01	.01	—	.01	.05	—
5) Willing to form JV	—	.10	—	—	—	—
6) Minority JV	$(.20)^2$	—	$(.05)^2$	—	—	—
7) Cost benefit JV	.15	—	—	—	—	—
8) Contingency plans	.15	.05	—	.05	.10	.15
9) Making the venture work	—	—	—	.20	—	—
10) MNE willing to visit	.01	.01	.15	.11	.05	—
11) Commit resources	.15	—	—	—	—	.05
12) Special skills	.10	.01	—	.01	.05	.05
13) Will change procedures	(.10)	—	—	—	—	—
14) Regular meetings	.05	.05	—	.20	.20	—
15) All discussions	.05	.10	—	—	—	—
16) Additional time	—	—	—	—	—	—

Notes:

1) Kolmogorov-Smirnov One-Sample Test used to derive significance levels.

2) Bracketed numeric values indicate that this statement is uncharacteristic of the respondents; unbracketed values indicate the statement is characteristic.

Items 1, 2, 14, 16 relate to commitment to international business
Items 3, 4, 5, 6 relate to commitment to the joint venture structure
Items 7, 8, 10, 13 relate to commitment to the particular joint venture
Items 9, 11, 12, 15 relate to commitment to the particular partner.

4.5 DISCUSSION

The results obtained indicate that the existence of commitment may be a very important ingredient in achieving high levels of JV performance. In this section we review in greater detail the specific commitment characteristics that were found to be significantly related to performance. These are summarised in Table 4.2.

Characteristics of commitment

a) Commitment to international business

i) The parent company is quite willing to adapt product to the needs of the local market. This statement was considered characteristic of the multinational executives from the high- but not low-performing ventures. It is considered to be a useful measure of commitment to international business since it was hypothesised that those firms with an international orientation would be most willing to take steps with their product line to satisfy local market needs. Examples of product adaptation include product reformulation to account for local tastes and package-size changes to account for local preferences.

ii) We have made a strong effort to increase the number of nationals employed in the venture. This statement was considered to be a potential indicator of commitment to international business because of the strong emphasis placed on staffing issues by both foreign and local partners. Like the previous statement, this was considered characteristic (.01 significance) of the multinational executives from the high- but not low-performing ventures. In fact, in several of the successful ventures, the MNE parents noted that they wished the expatriates they were using in other ventures were as competent as the local joint-venture general manager. This statement was neither characteristic nor uncharacteristic of the multinational executives from low-performing ventures.

In all of the high-performing ventures the general manager was a national of the local country. In fact, in most cases, the general manager was also the partner. In contrast, in a majority of the low-performing ventures, there was either an expatriate general manager or a significant expatriate presence. In several cases, the multinational executives from the low-performing joint ventures were concerned that, if the general managers were from the local country, the government might attempt to play off their nationalist tendencies in such a way that they would put the country's interests ahead of the company's. To this end, some foreign firms always like to have at least one expatriate present in their joint ventures. The general-manager respondents, and especially those who held equity, agreed that a strong effort had been made to increase the number of nationals employed in the venture.

We can speculate that this use of expatriates, rather than qualified local managers, results in a lack of MNE knowledge of the local economy, politics and customs, which in turn translates into poor performance. Certainly, the unwillingness on the part of some multinationals to find or develop qualified local managers — when other companies in the same country and industry were able to do so — demonstrates a lower commitment to international business.

b) Commitment to the joint-venture structure

i) The parent company is quite willing to take a minority equity position in a joint venture. The multinational executives from the low-performing ventures rated this statement as uncharacteristic of themselves. They were unwilling to take a minority equity position unless they were able to structure the venture holdings in such a way that they were still the single largest shareholder, or could have the management contract. As one executive noted, 'If we can't have a controlling interest, why put a lot of cash in?' Insistence on dominant ownership seems ill conceived in LDCs. By not explicitly recognising the benefits of shared ownership and control, many MNEs are setting the stage for poor performance.

Also, in several cases, foreign parent companies were acquired by other multinationals that had different policies towards the use of joint ventures. The newly imposed policies led in one case to the parent company being forced to convert its ventures to wholly owned subsidiaries — with disastrous results.

ii) The parent company has contingency plans for providing its joint ventures with increased levels of assistance if necessary. The multinational executives from the high-performing ventures in particular (.05 significance), rated this statement as being characteristic of themselves. In most cases, however, these contingency plans were not particularly comprehensive. The equity-holding general managers credited the multinational executives with being more likely to have these contingency plans than the executives credited themselves. This suggests that the multinational executives have successfully created the impression with their general managers that they are more committed to the use of joint ventures than they are in fact. Since the contingency plans were not always formalised, this could imply that general managers — many of whom are from the local country — may have greater scope than they realise in influencing the direction of the joint venture when problems arise.

c) Commitment to the particular joint venture

i) Management from the parent company is quite willing to visit regularly and offer assistance to the joint venture. The multinational executives almost unanimously agreed (.01 significance) that they were willing to visit regularly and offer assistance to the joint venture. Only one executive acknowledged that they have not been as willing to visit 'as much as we should'. (The MNE-appointed general manager of the venture attributed the rarity of parent visits to 'confidence in local management'.) One other executive noted that they will offer assistance 'provided it isn't money'. The general managers as a group also agreed that the foreign parent company (although one locally supplied GM took issue with the term 'foreign parent' company) was willing to visit regularly and offer assistance to the joint venture.

For some of the ventures we can speculate that this willingness to visit the joint venture was related to their tropical locales. A number of MNE executives acknowledged the opportunity to combine business and vacation through a visit to the venture. One regional manager cynically noted that, 'the entire royal corporate entourage goes if it's a nice place to visit'.

ii) When special skills are required by the joint venture, we try to first find them in the parent organisation. The multinational executives from the high-performing ventures indicated that this statement was characteristic. However, some of the MNE executives noted that they hoped their local partners and general managers would first look locally when special skills were required by the joint venture. The general managers were unanimous in looking to the parent organisation first when special skills were required — yet another example of the different ways in which the main players in each venture view their roles.

d) Commitment to the particular venture partner

i) We try to ensure through regular meetings that each partner knows what to expect from the joint venture. The multinational executives as a group, and those from the high-performing ventures in particular (.05 significance), considered this statement to be characteristic. The general managers as a group, and those holding equity in particular (.20 significance), also considered this statement to be characteristic. In four of the five cases where the statement was assessed 3 or lower (on the 5-point scale) by the MNE executive or his general manager, the venture was a low-performer. This relationship between low performance and low commitment to the partner points out the clear benefits to maintaining regular communication between the partners. In fact, some managers emphasised the importance of trust. One executive pointed out, 'The climate of trust between the partners is much more important than what is in the joint-venture agreement. (At the same time, the agreement should be a tight one as this is ultimately in everyone's best interests.) Trust is important because there is always an element of tension due to the possibility of a stalemate in the decision-making process.'

4.6 COMMITMENT SUMMARY

Four statements were characteristic (.05 significance) of the MNE respondents in aggregate: i) Management from the parent company is quite willing regularly to visit and offer assistance to the joint venture; ii) We try to ensure that through regular meetings each partner knows what to expect from the joint venture; iii) We try to include our partner even in those discussions which the management agreement says we can handle ourselves; and iv) We have made a strong effort to increase the number of nationals employed in the venture. No statements were deemed uncharacteristic of the multinational executives as a group.

Only one statement was classed as uncharacteristic and this was by the multinational executives from the low-performing ventures. The uncharacteristic statement was: 'The parent company is quite willing to take a minority equity position in a joint venture.'

Conversely, there was a total of six statements (Table 4.1) that the executives from the high-, but not the low-performing ventures considered to be characteristic. Three of these six statements were also considered characteristic of the aggregate group of ventures. For each of the four levels of commitment (to international business, to the use of joint ventures, to the particular venture, and to the particular parent), there was at least one statement that was characteristic of MNE executives from the high-performing ventures at a .05 or lower significance level.

4.7 CONCLUSIONS

Virtually all firms were capable of being committed to any or all of international business, the use of joint ventures, a particular venture, or a particular joint venture partner. There is nothing mysterious about commitment. Most of the commitment characteristics in the high-performing ventures were related to the MNEs willingness to do something: adapt products, increase employment of nationals, visit and offer assistance, or supply special skills. Commitment was not precluded because of a firm's inability to undertake these activities.

Commitment is seldom anything which is instantly created but must develop over time. In the foreign investment decision process, Aharoni (1966) felt the very act of collecting information created many individual commitments, and often organisational ones as well. Aharoni noted that in order to collect information it is necessary to communicate with people, to make certain decisions, and often to give tacit promises. In this process, commitments are accumulated. While the collection of information forms part of the basis for 'getting' commitment, the managers in a firm will not be willing to go to the trouble of changing behaviour (i.e. adapting products, employing nationals, forming joint ventures, holding regular meetings, etc.) unless they genuinely believe that they will derive a benefit from such activities.

Once commitment is developed, however, it often takes on the status of a corporate value. Thus, while initial projects tend to receive a fairly rational cost/benefit analysis of their feasibility, later projects are more influenced by existing corporate attitudes. For example, if past corporate experience with joint ventures has been negative, it is unlikely that a firm will demonstrate much commitment to subsequent projects. Although these behaviours had a tendency to become entrenched, getting or increasing commitment was always possible.

Not surprisingly, there was a strong correlation between the commitment results and several other constructs — specifically control and need — from Chapters 2 and 3. Those firms exhibiting a willingness to be flexible and undertake a particular activity (commitment) were likely to be the same firms favouring a sharing of decision-making (control) and looking for greater contributions (need) from their partners.

This chapter has noted the positive association with performance of MNEs using local management, being willing to use voluntarily the joint-venture structure, of looking to the local partner for his knowledge of the local economy, politics and culture; and having shared decision-making control. Assuming the existence of a legitimate business opportunity, joint ventures can be successfully employed in LDCs. However, all too often, one or both partners do not allocate sufficient effort to make the business a success. There is no secret formula for joint venture success: it ultimately partially comes down to whether there is an on-going commitment from the people involved.

NOTE

*An earlier version of this chapter appeared in the Proceedings of the 1986 International Conference on Marketing and Development and is reproduced with permission.

5

A Management Guideline for Joint Ventures in Developing Countries*

5.1 INTRODUCTION

Although joint ventures are extremely common in LDCs they frequently do not meet performance expectations. The executives we have surveyed were dissatisfied with the performance of more than half of their international joint ventures. None was totally satisfied with all their joint ventures.

Executives often prefer wholly-owned subsidiaries because these can ensure headquarters control and simplify organisational relationships. However, there are many compelling reasons to use joint ventures. Pressure from host governments for local equity participation in ventures is common. In some LDCs, joint ventures with local businessmen are the only means available for investment. Host governments want local involvement in the industrial base of their countries, jobs created and a transfer of technology. This is unlikely to change.

Even if not coerced into a joint venture, companies may use them to achieve what appear to be important benefits, including:

1) Faster and easier access to the local market and the distribution system;
2) Improved knowledge of the local economy, politics and culture;
3) Improved access to local human resources, including managers and labour;
4) A sharing of risk;
5) Preferential treatment. This could include the repatriation of dividends, the registering of investment to increase the

57

capital base on which dividends may be computed, and the securing of government contracts and work permits for expatriates.

The anticipated benefits may never be achieved. Our basic observation is that the problems of joint ventures are related not so much to strategy formulation, but primarily to poor implementation, and to lack of management attention after the venture has started operating. The potential benefits of joint ventures are real, but not guaranteed.

There is no simple formula for achieving success with joint ventures in LDCs. But, there are a series of conditions and processes which we believe improve a firm's prospect for success. This chapter will address the reasons why multinationals experience joint venture performance problems and will provide some guidelines for managers assessing joint ventures in the majority of developing countries — those with market, or mixed, economies.

5.2 JOINT VENTURE PROCESS

Problems that eventually may debilitate a joint venture can develop at any point in the process. There are four areas where managers need to be particularly vigilant. We have seen recurring patterns associated with eventual performance difficulties in each of the four: the decision to form the venture, partner selection, the design of the organisation, and the ongoing relationship between the partners.

5.3 THE DECISION TO FORM THE VENTURE

It is important to understand clearly why the company wants a joint venture. Many joint ventures are poorly conceived and probably should not be formed. We have encountered several which were created as a result of an inaccurate perception of government pressure to form the venture, and others in which a firm agreed to a joint venture in a peripheral business to which it had no commitment.

In some cases, the internal evaluation and reward systems of a corporation may encourage, unduly, the formation of joint ventures. Expansion-oriented companies may overemphasise 'beating the bushes' for new areas of operations. Returning home with a signed joint-venture contract may satisfy the executive's personal needs in relation to corporate evaluation systems. Also, it is human nature to want to show results from your investigative work, and to justify the costs of travel and market studies. Executives cannot keep travelling extensively without 'something to show for it'.

Two of the pressures we have seen on executives to conclude a deal expeditiously were managers' drive to achieve objectives set in the Management by Objective process and a corporation's desire to repatriate funds from the sale of stock converting a wholly-owned subsidiary to a minority joint venture prior to the year-end reports. The obvious implication is to ensure that evaluation and reward systems do not 'force' executives to make hasty decisions in support of poorly conceived objectives.

Too often, entering into a joint venture is a result of organisational and individual pressures rather than for good strategic or economic reasons. Euphemistically regarding a venture as a 'sharing of risks', may only be delaying the day that it is recognised as a bad deal. Strategic and economic benefits are crucial first considerations. However, they are analogous to the proverbial 'tip of the iceberg'. Implementation and operating difficulties lie hidden below the surface.

5.4 ASSESSING THE COMPANY AS A JOINT VENTURER

Even if there are sound strategic and economic reasons, the company may lack the necessary skills and qualities to implement the strategy and to be a good joint venturer. An MNE's capability and commitment to function in the joint venture mode must be realistically assessed. This assessment likely will provide insight into how the MNE will respond in the difficult situations that undoubtedly will be encountered. The initial question is extremely important, but deceptively simple: is the company really serious? The first indication of whether or not the company is likely to be a successful joint venturer is its commitment to international business and to working in LDCs. Does the company have the capacity and staying power to realise the anticipated pay-off? Rational strategies have a way of deteriorating as executives encounter the practical difficulties common in LDCs and become frustrated.

Before entering into a joint venture in a developing country, firms must make a conscious decision that they want to be in that country and that the company belongs there. There is a need to recognise that developing business in the Third World is a long-term proposition and investment. As well, overseas travel is expensive and negotiations are slow. Managers cannot be impatient. If expectations are otherwise, it is an early indication of future problems.

There are personal pressures to act quickly, and the potential for mistakes in the name of efficiency is enormous. Some executives also may have a concomitant attitude of superiority. In addition managers often do not like conditions in the developing world. They want to get out. So they push to complete a project or resolve a partnership issue more quickly than they should.

Some companies would prefer to limit their degree of adaptation, preferring the use of wholly-owned subsidiaries, and staffing with expatriates rather than nationals. In our opinion, the best joint venturers — meaning those who work towards ensuring the long-term viability of the business — are the companies that recognise their specific long-term needs and recruit partners to fill these needs. Specifically, they look to their partner for general knowledge of the local economy, politics and culture, and for the supply of general managers. They also recognise the tangible and intangible costs associated with an early dissolution.

5.5 SELECTING A PARTNER

Identifying and selecting a partner is possibly the most important consideration in establishing a joint venture (Geringer, 1986). It also may be the most difficult and time-consuming. Even though partner selection could be the determining factor in success or failure, it may not be given the time and attention that it deserves. The most common problems cited with joint ventures in LDCs involve the local partner.

A number of firms we have encountered were impatient to find a partner and to enter an attractive market. As a result, they were careless in their selection process and mistakenly traded poor partner quality for quick action. Partners are often selected only for short-term and political reasons. When these characteristics are no longer useful and the partner has nothing else to offer, the relationship often ends.

There are three issues to consider: what characteristics to look for in a partner, where to locate a potential partner, and how to know whether or not you have made the right choice.

In the unsuccessful ventures in the Caribbean, the MNE primarily looked for a partner to satisfy existing or expected government requirements for local ownership. This is a short-term orientation. Companies can be trapped by short-term thinking and expedient action. The temptation may be great to have a local politician or government official as a joint venture partner. However, a partner should be expected to bring more to the partnership than position or contacts. He should be able to make a contribution to the ongoing operation.

In the successful ventures, the MNEs looked for partners to provide general knowledge of the local economy, politics and culture, and to provide managers. They viewed these as ongoing and long-term needs. Corporations may think that local knowledge is a short-term need and that the company will learn quickly. Our experience suggests that the local scene keeps changing. New players appear, as well as new attitudes, regulations and laws. Learning must keep pace. Expatriates living in the country are often out of touch with the country and culture. They become insulated from reality by the expatriate community. The research in the Caribbean indicated that the acquisition of information about local conditions, and understanding of them was the most important long-term need. Local people can fill this need best.

Generally speaking, local governments are inappropriate partners because they cannot supply good general managers to the joint venture. In addition, governments are motivated by considerations other than performance, such as providing social benefits. A need to provide employment, for example, may be inconsistent with the joint venture's needs. Many executives reported that they avoid joint ventures with governments if at all possible.

The best advice seems to be: use industrialists of some stature in the same or a similar business — if you can find them. The next best choice would be a firm that offers a complementary service such as product distribution. As you move further from your business base, the ability of your partner to contribute substantially to the venture and to provide qualified general managers declines.

Finding the right partner easily can take a year or more and there is no substitute for active, rigorous exploration. As we talk with executives, we are continually amazed at how some partners have been found. Some have been met 'fortuitously' at cocktail parties in Latin America or Trinidad, or in a hotel bar in Nigeria. Non-rigorous search may result in taking the first partner who comes along, which most likely is a mistake.

Beware the tendency to confuse an introduction for a recommendation. An introduction to a casual acquaintance is all too frequently mistaken for a personal recommendation. The person setting up the introduction often has good credentials, such as being a banker or diplomat, and these sometimes artificially legitimise the contact.

Take advantage of serendipity, but recognise that a chance meeting is only the beginning. Visit your potential partner in his milieu. See how he lives and how he runs his business; and have him do the same with you. We also would suggest trying to find ways in which to work together on smaller projects to 'test' the working relationship. It is easier and more satisfactory to increase investment in a small project than to write off one's large investment.

It is essential to establish clearly the motivation and expectations of both parties. We have talked to companies which expected their partners to be actively involved in the joint venture and were disappointed when they were not. Others expected to have silent partners and were upset when the partners became active. Expectations can only be clarified with time; by focusing on the issue directly; and by being sensitive to potential misunderstandings due to differences in culture.

Geringer (1986) has noted how size differentials can create problems. Large MNEs tend to be systematic and slow in their decision-making. They also may have a long-term, investment orientation and a willingness to reap rewards in the future. In contrast, their partner may be an entrepreneur who manages intuitively and makes decisions very quickly. Such a partner more likely will have immediate financial needs.

The partner selection process often involves interaction with prominent families in LDCs. Very often the culture of these countries dictates putting family interests ahead of rational business development. Every family is made up of individuals with varying qualifications. There is a need to be sure you know with whom in the family you will be working.

MNEs often have to face the issue of multiple business

interests on the part of their partners. Firms may be scared away from an excellent partner because of the partner's seemingly unfocused diversity of interests. However, it is a legitimate concern that such interests will dilute the partner's attention to your joint venture unless a solid management team is put into place. This is an area in which expectations must be established clearly.

Once a partner has been chosen and the joint venture is established, the real work begins. A successful relationship requires constant attention and nourishing. As one executive explained, 'Good private partners have to be cherished and taken care of.' He was not talking about doing anything illegal either. His company invests heavily in travel and communications to maintain its personal relationships.

5.6 MUTUAL NEED AND COMMITMENT

To be successful, a partnership must operate on the principle of fair exchange. There must be value in the relationship for both parties. Multinationals should be willing to interact regularly with their local partners. A partnership probably should not be established unless there is a strong likelihood of cooperation and ongoing two-way communication. As discussed in Chapters 3 and 4, major differences in the performance of joint ventures in developing countries relate to whether there exists a long-term need and commitment between the partners. When there is, the ventures are more likely to be stable and successful.

Commitment is necessary for success and is required at each step in the process. Commitment is required to overcome initial uncertainties associated with a new country or partner. One executive with a highly successful international corporation has stated: 'Commitment is probably the single most critical factor for successful entry into foreign markets.' He referred specifically to many facets of commitment: financial commitment; commitment to customer and partner support; to product integrity; to company employees around the world; to understanding the politics, economics and culture of trading partners; to the building of trust and sharing of information; to the building of cooperative relationships.

Commitment has also been characterised as a challenge. Commitment is built and becomes an important value in a corporation. Without commitment, the numerous problems that come with the 'territory' of joint ventures and developing countries can become overwhelming and provide a reason for quitting: the venture is requiring more attention and resources than expected or forecast, and no longer looks as good as it did at the start.

Commitment is probably the most important attribute in the ongoing management of a joint venture. A sense of duty to the venture and partner is the basis on which problems are addressed and solved, changes made and help provided.

To be successful, it is important both to need a local partner and be committed to the joint venture. One company's entry into Nigeria required nearly ten years of very difficult work to make the joint venture a success. Much as the MNE felt it needed a local partner, however, it seems doubtful whether the venture would have succeeded without a long-term commitment to problem-solving as well. This outcome is not surprising since this company had developed the minority joint venture as a *modus operandi* in the developing world. It had invested in learning how to operate profitably in this mode.

Many other firms do not. Some MNEs take one of two extreme positions with their local partners. In the first instance, the MNE takes an arm's-length investment approach to the joint venture. The MNE is reluctant to visit the joint venture when problems arise and is unwilling to supply special skills to the venture from the parent organisation if they are needed.

In the second extreme, an MNE manages the joint venture but tends to operate as if it were a wholly-owned subsidiary. The local partner is not kept informed or involved in decision-making. The MNE does not like to hold regular meetings and is only willing to include the local partner in discussions if the management contract specifies that they are obligatory. In each of these extremes, the MNE has forgotten that it is a joint venture and that both partners have something to contribute.

5.7 DESIGNING THE VENTURE

Decisions must be made about the equity structure, how and by whom the venture will be staffed and who has decision-making responsibility in specific areas. Decision-making control can either be shared, or dominated by one of the partners. In LDCs, shared decision-making control is recommended.

The concept of shared control — especially *how* to do it — is confusing to some managers. Even if they support shared control in principle, they cannot see how to put it into practice. Shared control conjures up an image of two or more people making every decision, no matter how small. They fear that, at a minimum, decision-making will be excessively slow; and worse, that it will break down altogether.

Shared control is not, as some managers fear, a variation on the organisational bugaboo — the matrix structure. Even when decisions are shared within a joint venture, they are in fact frequently not being jointly made but rather divided or split between the partners based on knowledge, skill, experience and understanding of the particular issue. An element of specialisation is maintained. The foreign partner may have a better understanding of the technology and the local partner a clearer grasp of the local market and political conditions. However, since there is an interaction between product and market there must be an interaction between partners. Some decisions will have to be jointly made, arrived at through consensus after discussions. Not to do so ignores the other's expertise. More of the decisions are likely to be made by one partner or the other, as agreed upon at the time of the joint venture formation, when the expectations and contributions of each should be made explicit.

Consensus decision-making takes time and creates potential conflict situations. However, since it is not every decision that must be made this way it is not an onerous requirement. It may not be as efficient allowing one partner to make all the decisions but, we believe, it is more effective. However, it requires people who are sensitive to the partner's needs and culture and who are willing to understand, learn and be persuaded, as well as being persuasive. Managing successfully in a minority joint venture seems to imply a shift from control through the financial structure to influence through creating relationships and through behavioural interaction.

Firms should hire the best available local lawyer and accounting firm to help with the legal and financial structuring of the partnership agreement. The lawyers and accountants should codify the basic operating agreement already made by the principals to the joint venture, and not determine that agreement. One executive went so far as to say that these people should not be involved until the general agreement and expectations have been made clear by the principals and their commitment to functioning as a joint venture also has been made.

65

The use of local managers rather than expatriates is recommended, to ensure the MNE acquires the necessary knowledge of the local economy, politics and culture. As one international vice-president noted, 'In many LDCs it takes about 20 years to really understand the local system — and we just can't leave our (expatriate) managers there that long.' Two additional reasons cited for using local managers are their lower costs, and the increasing supply of competent local managers.

Although the supply of competent local managers is increasing, the demand for such managers is high. The solution for many companies has been to offer equity to the general manager (and in some cases to other senior local managers). This not only improves the probability of maintaining a qualified management team but also provides motivation for good performance.

It is recommended that MNEs take a minority or equal amount of equity. The actual equity positions of each partner do not necessarily reflect their respective levels of influence. Ownership is not the same as control. Although most MNEs have a minority equity position in their LDC-based joint ventures, they are often able to maintain an equal voice in the operations of the business. With a general manager and other senior local managers holding equity, the MNE can be the single largest shareholder and still be in a minority equity position. Minority equity does not mean the MNE will have a minority voice in the joint venture's operations, and preferential treatment may result if it is equally or majority-owned by locals.

5.8   ONGOING MANAGEMENT AND RELATIONSHIP

The real work begins after the decision has been made to establish the joint venture, a partner has been selected, and the management structure decided upon. Contractual obligations must be met; the personal relationship with the partner maintained and nurtured; and problems solved.

Many MNEs are involved with joint ventures that are currently performing poorly or likely will soon experience difficulties. When problems arise, many of these MNEs will blame their partner, the local government, the general state of the economy — in fact, almost anyone or anything except themselves. Yet, there is evidence to suggest that they should look internally for the explanation.

Table 5.1: Summary guideline for implementing a joint venture strategy in developing countries

Consider forming a joint venture when the MNE:	Proceed with partner selection	When establishing, designing and operating the venture:
i) Has ascertained the economic and strategic contribution	i) After a rigorous search has been conducted	i) Use local managers
ii) Is committed to international business, particularly in developing countries	ii) After expectations are clarified	ii) Sell equity to the general manager
iii) Is committed to the use of joint ventures, including minority joint ventures	iii) When the partner has a long-term need for the MNE	iii) Take an equal or minority amount of equity
iv) Has a long-term need for specific partner contributions	iv) When there is a commitment to the particular venture and the partner	iv) Use shared decision-making
		v) Invest in maintaining the relationship

Of the many joint ventures we investigated, several involved the turnaround of poor performers. In every case, among the changes made by the MNE was a rethinking of their attitudes towards the value of local partners. Accompanying these turn-arounds was the recognition that the local partner was needed for specific contributions and that sharing the decision-making might, after all, make sense.

5.9 CASES IN CONTRAST: SUCCESS AND FAILURE

A summary guideline for implementing a joint venture in

developing countries is shown in Table 5.1 and a comparison of a successful and unsuccessful venture follows. In our minds, a successful joint venture is a stable, healthy and profitable business relationship that meets the needs of both partners. Success should be viewed as a mutual condition, not a one-sided one.

The two joint ventures, which we have called Alpha and Beta, were established in the Caribbean. They were remarkably similar in their product-market strategies and their sales volume, but quite different in their joint-venture strategies. Both produced primarily for the local market and had high (50 per cent) market shares. The firms were not direct competitors.

Each was a joint venture between a foreign company (Canadian and American respectively) and a private local firm. Both of the private local firms were well established and had previous experience with MNEs. Both companies had annual sales in excess of $1 billion and also had previous experience in LDCs and with joint ventures. Both MNEs were earning a 20 per cent return on equity (ROE) and were satisfied with the performance of their respective joint ventures. Unlike the Alpha venture, however, the local partner in Beta was dissatisfied with the joint venture for a number of reasons which included, but were not limited to, financial considerations.

5.10 INVESTING IN LDCs USING THE JOINT-VENTURE ORGANISATION FORM

In the Alpha venture, the MNE partner never considered using a wholly-owned subsidiary, even though there was no government pressure to use the joint venture organisation form. Early progress was slow while a local general manager was found. The MNE partner believed that increasing the number of nationals employed, especially in managerial positions, would not only demonstrate greater commitment to the local community but that it also made sound business sense. The parent company recognised that it lacked knowledge of the local economy, politics and culture, and wanted the local partner and local general manager for this reason. An immediate payoff came in the area of plant construction: the plant was completed ahead of schedule and 18 per cent below budgeted cost. The generally accepted explanation for the cost savings was that because the general manager was a national with local knowledge, he was able to obtain the best price from local contractors.

Until the early 1970s, the MNE partner in the Beta venture had been importing into the Caribbean. When its major competitor, a European importer, approached the local government about establishing a manufacturing plant, the company was forced to act. The local government was offering a five-year tax holiday and imposing limitations on imports as well. However, it wanted only one local manufacturer. On the basis of their better-known brand name, the North American company was awarded the franchise for local production.

Because it anticipated government requirements for local ownership or some other form of government intervention, the firm decided to form a joint venture, even though it would have preferred a wholly-owned subsidiary. As a reluctant joint venturer, its practice was to staff senior positions with expatriates and to look for a partner with government contacts. The MNE wanted a partner who could assist in obtaining work permits for foreign executives.

5.11 SELECTING A PARTNER

In the Alpha venture, commitment to the local partner was demonstrated by holding regular meetings, often informally over lunch, even when there were no agenda items. This was in direct contrast to the Beta venture, where the MNE-supplied expatriate general manager felt it was unnecessary to include the local partner in any discussions which the management agreement said the foreign partner could handle itself. Not surprisingly, the local partner in the Alpha venture felt his foreign partner trusted him, the local partner in the Beta venture did not. As the local partner in the Beta venture noted, 'If you feel your partner does not trust you, little differences tend to aggravate situations.'

5.12 DESIGNING THE VENTURE

In the Alpha venture, all of the managers were from the local country. Although the general manager did not hold equity in the venture, all sides were in agreement that this would be

69

desirable and steps were being taken in this direction. The North American company in this venture holds 40 per cent of the equity and shares decision-making with the local partner. Both partners are satisfied with performance.

In the Beta venture, the two senior managers are expatriates. The expatriate general manager does not hold an equity position. The North American partner has a majority (65 per cent) equity position. As well, the MNE partner has dominant control over decision-making, in fact operating the joint venture much like a wholly-owned subsidiary. The MNE-supplied general manager considers this approach to decision-making control appropriate since he feels the local partner views the joint venture only as an investment. Unfortunately, this is not how the local partner views his involvement. The local partner in the Beta venture feels that he knows the market and has a better plan for developing the company. To date, the MNE has not been receptive to suggestions.

There are four areas of conflict in the Beta venture: distributor arrangement, management contract, relative equity positions, and profits.

The major product produced by the venture is distributed by a wholly-owned subsidiary of the MNE. There have been major disagreements between the partners regarding the price at which production is sold to the distributor. The lower the price to the distributor, the greater the profit that the MNE partner does not have to share. The threat of similar non-arm's-length transactions was avoided in the Alpha venture by not guaranteeing distribution through the MNE's distribution company.

A second issue relates to the use of the management contract, which is a source of income to the partner to whom it is awarded. The local partner feels the length of management contracts (which until now have always been awarded to the MNE partner) should be shortened to provide some control over poor performance. In the Alpha venture, management fees were tied to productivity; in Beta, they were not.

A third issue was equity levels. The original agreement specified that the foreign partner would ultimately reduce its equity position from 65 per cent to 45 per cent, with the local partner increasing his holding to 45 per cent, and ten per cent being sold to other local interests. For the past two years, the local partner has been asking the MNE to negotiate a price for this equity transfer; however, 'they have been tardy in coming to a conclusion'. The MNE partner readily acknowledges its reluctance to be a minority-equity partner.

The final issue is profits. Although the MNE is earning a 20 per cent ROE from a variety of sources within the business, the local partner, with dividends as his sole source of income, is earning less than ten per cent ROE. The local partner notes that his 'patience over profits is running out'. In the Alpha venture, both partners had similar earnings.

5.13 MAJOR DIFFERENCES

The Alpha joint venture was entered into voluntarily by the foreign MNE. It wanted a partner with local knowledge; it maintained regular communication with the partner; and it shared the decision-making and profits. Both partners were satisfied with Alpha's performance and its prospects for continued success.

The Beta joint venture was entered into pre-emptively by the foreign MNE. It wanted a local partner only because of a perception that it would be better off with the local government if it had one. No contribution was expected from the local partner for local market knowledge or managers. No specific need for, or commitment to, the local partner was demonstrated by the MNE. The local partner was dissatisfied with this arrangement. This joint venture had significant problems to resolve in order to survive.

NOTE

*This chapter was co-authored by Henry W. Lane. An earlier version appeared as a Working Paper at the University of Western Ontario.

6

Joint Venture General Managers*

With the prevalence of joint ventures in LDCs, the demand for joint venture general managers (JVGMs) has increased. Life as the head of a joint venture is characterised by a unique tension inherent to this particular organisational form. Double parenting exacerbates the difficulties and challenges that are a normal part of managing internationally, and also creates new ones.

The JVGM's role differs from that of general manager in a wholly-owned subsidiary. His task is more complicated in a variety of ways: with essentially two bosses and two sets of expectations, he must simultaneously accommodate the interests of two partners. He often faces a great deal of ambiguity in terms of defining both parents' criteria of success and must deal with issues of commitment and communication between the two parents. At the same time he has less job security — if either parent or the board of directors disapproves of him, he may well have to move.

Amongst all these disadvantages, the JVGM does have several things to look forward to. He has two sets of resources and skills with which to work. He can often produce at better economies than competitors in the LDC by gaining quality and technical expertise from the MNE and knowledge of the local economy, politics and culture from the local partner. A framework developed by Mintzberg (1980) provides a brief overview of the JVGM's role as compared to that of the general manager of a wholly-owned subsidiary (WOS) in a foreign country and a wholly-owned subsidiary in its home country (Table 6.1).

The role of the JVGM is to balance these opportunities and

Table 6.1: Role of the general manager (GM): three perspectives

1 As they apply to GM of WOS in a DC[1]	2 As they apply to GM of WOS in an LDC	3 As they apply to GM of JV in an LDC
Interpersonal roles		
1) Figurehead role — represents the organisation on ceremonial occasions	As in column 1; however additional legal requirements in each country necessitate greater emphasis in this role	As in column 2 plus increased number of occasions due to ceremonial situations relating to two nationalities
2) Liaison role — interacting with other managers and groups outside the organisation unit	Very prominent; must also frequently interact with government officials; may have problems if GM is an expatriate and working/dealing with nationals outside organisational unit	As in column 2
3) Leader role — establishing relationships with subordinates (motivating, supervising) and exercising formal authority within the organisational unit	More complex than in 1; may find it difficult to motivate and supervise nationals due to different values and ethics, etc	Increased complexity compared to 2; must do this with expatriates and nationals likely from different countries; hence, must understand how to motivate people from other countries
Information roles		
1) Monitor role — receiving and collecting information from both inside and outside the organisational unit	Outside information-searching may be harder for an expatriate in an LDC than a DC; dealing with subordinates who are nationals may be hard	This is more easily done here as JVGM and managers may have access to information from two organisations
2) Disseminator role — transmitting information to members within the organisational unit	Can talk to nationals, but general manager is usually an expatriate, therefore may have communication breakdown	General manager usually national himself, hence role is easier

— continued overleaf

Table 6.1: — *continued*

1 As they apply to GM of WOS in a DC[1]	2 As they apply to GM of WOS in an LDC	3 As they apply to GM of JV in an LDC
Information roles		
3) Spokesman role — informing those outside the organisational unit	Again, due to being expatriate, often difficult to do	Being national, it would be easier to do; however more groups (partners) for information to be conveyed to
Decision-related roles		
1) Innovator role — initiating change	Easier than JVGM due to need to convince only one superior; more complex than in 1 since physical distance means GM cannot rely on others	Very prominent role; must convince both parents and the board of directors (BOD)
2) Resource allocation — deciding where efforts and energies will be directed	Similar to 1; not too difficult since there would be one set of objectives to achieve rather than conflicting goals as in 3	Very difficult due to two sets of resources and expectations
3) Negotiator role — dealing with situations involving negotiations on behalf of the organisation	Due to being expatriate may be difficult; as well, presence in an LDC environment may complicate negotiations	Perhaps the primary skill required of the JVGM
4) Disturbance handler role — taking charge when crises arise and the organisation is threatened	Handles individually; support from direct superior if need be, but as above	Has other influences (both parents and BOD) which complicate the decision

Note: 1. This column from Mintzberg.

risks and make them work for him. Achievement of this difficult task can make for a successful venture.

The purpose of this chapter is to analyse the unique features of joint-venture general management in LDCs. It begins with the identification and discussion of the major pressures which determine the JVGM's strategic and operating context. It then examines how JVGMs respond to those pressures. The chapter concludes with a discussion of the implications of the study's findings for JVGMs, managers in parent organisations and researchers.

6.1 METHODOLOGY

This research is derived from two larger studies conducted by the authors (Schaan, 1983; Beamish, 1984) which involved in total nearly 75 joint ventures in LDCs.

Schaan conducted 39 personal interviews in four countries: Canada, Mexico, the US and France. As noted earlier, Beamish conducted 46 interviews in Canada, the US, the United Kingdom and two Caribbean nations. Questionnaires were used in some instances to supplement the interview observations.

Data for this chapter were obtained primarily from personal interviews with managers involved in 22 core joint ventures. In most cases interviews involved managers at three levels: the JVGM, multinational parent (MNE) representative and LDC parent representative. In total, 17 JVGMs were personally interviewed.

The MNE parent held a majority position in four JVs, six JVs were 50-50 and the MNE parent held a minority position in twelve JVs.

Twelve JVs were managed at the time of study by a JVGM appointed by the MNE parent. Among them, six were nationals from the MNE's country, four were local nationals and two were third country nationals. The JVGMs of the other ten JVs were appointed by the local parent and four of them were the local parent himself.

Of the 22 core joint ventures, seven were successful, nine were unsuccessful and six had been turned around. Half operated in Mexico, with all but one of the balance located in the Caribbean.

The performance of the JVs by ownership category is presented in Table 6.2. The data suggest that the JVs where the MNE holds a minority position have greater chances of success than where it holds a majority position.

Among the unsuccessful JVs, two-thirds were staffed with expatriates and one-third with local nationals, while the

75

proportions are reversed for the successful JVs — two-thirds are managed by local JVGMs and one-third is managed by expatriates. Hence, a local JVGM seems to have greater chances of running a successful operation than an expatriate.

Table 6.2: Ownership and performance of sample JVs

	MNE majority %	50-50 %	MNE minority %
Successful	25	67	75
Unsuccessful	75	33	25

The core ventures were carefully selected to be representative of common types of joint venture in LDCs. All but one of the 22 ventures had been in operation for at least three years. Focus was placed on the manufacturing sector. Most of the ventures were in low-medium technology-intensive sectors such as food processing and production of non-durable consumer goods. All of the ventures were between a multinational enterprise from a developed country and a private local organisation from the LDC. Half of the firms exported, up to 25 per cent of sales.

The difficulty of securing cooperation from managers in LDCs plus the limited availability of joint ventures which met the specified requirements, meant that a pure random sample could not be employed. For example, Beamish employed a stratified sample in that where possible, both high and low performers in the same industry and same country were examined. Schaan in turn, used a convenience sample.

The core ventures had sales between US $1 million and $543 million. Average market share for the core ventures was 42 per cent, with a high standard deviation. The joint ventures had been in operation for an average of 11.5 years.

Only one of the core ventures had an effective monopoly position. In the other cases, either local manufacturing competition existed or tariffs were low enough to allow competitive imports.

The data analysis methods used included content analysis, frequency of response and non-parametric statistical tests such as the Kolmogorov-Smirnov One-Sample Test.

6.2 WHAT MAKES IT DIFFICULT TO MANAGE A JOINT VENTURE IN AN LDC?

Meeting the expectations of two parents

JVGMs tend to be evaluated on the basis of one, or a combination of, dimensions such as their ability to meet each parent's expectations, to achieve the joint venture's strategic objectives or simply to maintain a good working relationship with managers from parent organisations. A challenge facing JVGMs is not only that the parent organisations may have different sets of expectations, but more importantly that those expectations are seldom clearly communicated and that they change over time.

In 70 per cent of the joint ventures studied, JVGMs indicated that they had had in the past — or still had at the time of the interview — difficulties in understanding what the criteria of their parents were. In most cases the JVGM was not handed a clear set of criteria by his two parents. Typically, he had to learn over time, through a trial and error process, what he had to do well to make each parent happy.

The ambiguity thus created by the parents was in most cases unintended. However, in about ten per cent of the joint ventures studied, at least one of the parents was reluctant to make its expectations clear, fearing that it would weaken its bargaining power in its dealings with its partner.

Managers in parent organisations use a complex function of expectations in forming a judgement regarding how successful a joint venture is. They use a combination of quantitative (financial and economic) and qualitative criteria, with each criterion carrying a specific weight in the function. Further, both the criteria and the weights change over time. As a result JVGMs need to be perceptive enough to read the signals sent by managers from the parent companies, and adapt their personal and company's strategies to respond to changes in expectations.

Differences in the parents' expectations were found in the following areas:

In the dimensions used: e.g. growth *vs* ROI *vs* dividends;
In the time orientation: short-term *vs* long-term;
In the level of achievement: aggressiveness of the criteria; and
In the degree of specificity: undefined growth *vs* growth in sales of 20 per cent.

Managing a joint venture so as to meet two (or more) sets of expectations is a difficult task in itself. However it becomes an impossible one if the expectations are incompatible and there is no room or no willingness on the part of the parents to compromise. Joint ventures where this was the case did not survive very long.

It is difficult for a JVGM to meet all criteria for one parent simultaneously, let alone for two or more parents. Therefore managing a joint venture involves a subtle balancing act between the parents' priorities, the joint venture's strategic and operating priorities and the personal objectives, beliefs and values of the managers representing the various stakeholders in the joint venture. In most cases managers in the parent organisations had a satisficer's attitude towards the joint venture's performance. Such an attitude indicates that JVGMs have an opportunity to reach some sort of compromise which may be acceptable to the parents. Compromise is the rule rather than the exception in joint ventures; however, in the words of a Mexican manager, 'To ensure the long-term success of the joint venture, compromise must be perceived by all sides as being a mutual thing.'

Finally, the observed differences in expectations regarding 'good management practice' have been explained by Reynolds (1979) on the basis of the parents' attitudes towards the role of management in five areas: i) the source and the scope of the manager's authority; ii) status; iii) personality versus position; iv) responsibility for decision-making; and v) responsibility for future events.

Ensuring the economic viability of the joint venture

The joint-venture characteristic of greatest interest to both managers and researchers is performance. Since joint ventures are jointly owned, it is reasonable to examine whether both partners were satisfied with performance. Because one partner is a local firm and one is a foreign firm, we would expect differences in how performance might be assessed. In the country where the joint venture was located, the MNE partners were never strictly dependent on local earnings in determining their overall return. However, venture profits were often the only source of revenue for local partners, and as Reynolds (1979) notes, the joint venture was much more often the major industrial interest of the local partner. The foreign partner, therefore, might still be earning a good overall return from the business (i.e. through raw material sales, royalties, etc) when the venture itself was generating little, if any, profit. This did, in fact, occur in a number of cases.

In one case, the expatriate general manager claimed he could run it on a breakeven basis in the local country and the parent company would still find it lucrative. In this case, the local partner was not satisfied with the performance of the venture.

Those joint ventures in which at least one partner was unsatisfied with performance were considered unsatisfactory performers. Overall, of the 22 core ventures, 14 were classified as satisfactory performers using this system. In six of these cases, performance had been unsatisfactory but later turned around. In the eight unsatisfactory ventures, half were unsatisfactory from just one partner's perspective while the balance had either ceased operations or were performing poorly from both perspectives.

Joint managerial assessment was the sole performance measure used in the core ventures. Use of this measure is consistent with the way most JVGMs would assess performance. Nonetheless, one task of the JVGM is to continue reminding the parent company(ies) that there has to be *joint* satisfaction if the business is to remain viable.

Drawing from the partners' contributions

A mutual long-term need between joint-venture partners is another significant variable associated with the success of joint ventures. In Chapter 3, partner needs were categorised into five groups with three items in each group. These groups of needs were further broken down into long-term needs, short-term needs and unimportant needs according to three different perspectives: the MNEs in high-performing ventures, those in low-performing ventures, and the local general managers (Table 3.1 shows the correlation between the three perspectives and the three timeframes). This is a useful reference guide for JVGMs.

Local general managers deemed better export opportunities a need of long-term importance. As JVGMs, they wanted to see their ventures successful in the long run. Better export opportunities allowed the joint venture to increase sales and profits.

In the short term, local general managers hoped to gain raw material supply and technology or equipment from the parents. This is as one would expect since they are only beginning operations and need the assistance from the parents.

Local general managers noted four items as unimportant contributions from their parents: speed of entry into a country, local political advantages, inexpensive labour, and knowledge of the local economy, politics and culture. Given that two of the three of the foreign-supplied GMs had low-performing ventures, our view is that if these GMs had solicited feedback from the local partner they might have been more successful.

In the high-performing venture, the JVGM was a national of the local country and ranked this knowledge need low. This is a legitimate claim because as a national, he already would have the necessary background knowledge in this area.

Foreign-supplied GMs would do well to use local contributions. The JVGMs that have a successful venture look for contributions from the local parent.

JVGMs must be aware of their MNE parent's view on the importance of the local partner's contributions. By enabling the JVGM to see if the parent is acting as one would in a successful or unsuccessful venture, the JVGM can ensure the MNE parent realises the benefits to be gained from the local parent and use these assets to become or maintain its success.

This is key information for a JVGM. Knowing the importance of need and commitment a JVGM can act in a way to achieve the needed amounts of both to improve the prospects for joint-venture success. As intermediary, the JVGM can facilitate a trust relationship by involving the local partner in decisions affecting the joint venture even when there is no specific policy stated to involve the partner in a particular decision. By simply informing the partner on the activities of the joint venture, and involving him, the likelihood of success increases.

6.3 MANAGING IN AN ENVIRONMENT CONSTRAINED BY PARENT COMPANY CONTROL PRACTICES

The analysis of the parent companies' control practices shows that JVGMs generally have less autonomy than they want to think they have. In particular, joint ventures' boards of directors have been found to play a major role in the decision-making process, greater than in the joint ventures operating in developed countries. An explanation for this is that in LDCs, in addition to the level of uncertainty and the foreign parent's desire to be in control, there is a lack of managerial depth and the board of directors constitutes a mechanism for transferring the parents' expertise.

Control refers to the process through which a parent company assures that the way a joint venture is managed conforms with its own interests. From a JVGM's perspective, an understanding of the parents' control practices serves two purposes. First, it helps to map the boundaries of authority within which one is expected to operate; second, it helps to identify opportunities for independence (areas of freedom from parent authority or involvement).

Parent companies have been found to exercise control through both positive and negative mechanisms. A parent uses positive control when it is in a position to influence activities or decisions in a way consistent with its own expectations and interests. It uses negative control when it is in a position to prevent decisions or activities it does not agree with from being implemented (Table 6.3). Negative mechanisms such as a veto right over major decisions are particularly useful to parents in a minority shareholder position.

An analysis of the parent companies' control practices in joint ventures suggests that the autonomy of a JVGM is determined by how the following issues are actually implemented in a given case:

What JVGMs can/can't do. In all joint ventures there were decisions and/or activities that were unequivocally the responsibility of one parent, of both parents or of the JVGM. Of course, for many decisions the lines were not clearly defined. But for those decisions or activities that could be identified as being the prerogative of a given party to the joint venture, the allocation of authority was done in one of two ways.

First, the allocation was the result of negotiations during the planning phase of the joint venture and formally ratified in the joint venture agreement. This was the case for all the joint ventures studied. Differences existed regarding which decisions should be made by whom, depending on the area of expertise (e.g. technology, marketing) brought by a parent; or on the control policies of the parent (e.g. two large US multinationals had a

81

Table 6.3: Positive and negative control mechanisms

Positive	Negative
Ability to make specific decisions	Board
Ability to design:	Executive committee
1) Planning process	Approval required for:
2) Appropriation requests	1) Specific decision
	2) Plans, budgets
Policies and procedures	3) Appropriation requests
	4) Nomination JVGM
Ability to set objectives for JVGM	Screening/no objection of parent
Contracts: management	before ideas are discussed with
technology transfer	other parent
marketing	
supplier	
Participation in planning or	
budgeting process	
Parent organisation structure	
Reporting structure	
Staffing	
Training programme	
Staff services	
JVGM bonus tied to parent results	
Ability to decide on future	
promotion of JVGM (and other	
joint venture managers)	
Feedback: strategy/plan budgets,	
appropriation requests	
JVGM participation in parent's	
worldwide meetings	
Relations with JVGM: phone calls,	
meetings, visits	
Staffing parent with someone with	
experience with joint venture	
MNE level in the LDC	
Informal meetings with other	
parent	

Source: Schaan (1983), p. 249.

policy to appoint the finance manager and to make all operating financial decisions).

Second, the allocation could be the result of an implicit understanding and agreement of the parents regarding their respective territories of influence. This happened in cases where one parent would demonstrate greater expertise in a specific area than its partner or the JVGM.

What JVGMs need to get approval for and to whom JVGMs report. As in most companies, JVGMs had to get approval for their strategic and operating plans, their budgets, appointments of joint-venture top managers, capital budgeting decisions, etc. However, a distinctive characteristic of the joint ventures was that although JVGMs want to have a reporting relationship to the board, in 40 per cent of the Mexican joint ventures the JVGM had to clear specific issues with one parent before being allowed to discuss them with the other. Further, it was expected that no surprises would be brought up during the board meetings.

What JVGMs need to achieve, targets set by parents. In a minority of cases (20 per cent), JVGMs were given specific goals to achieve in terms of sales, profits or market share. However, in a greater number of cases (60 per cent) they were given very specific personal objectives such as conducting a market study or hiring and developing a new marketing manager.

Who sets policies and procedures and general management practices. In 70 per cent of the Mexican joint ventures, the joint venture's policies and procedures were a replication of one parent's. Since in each of those cases the JVGM had been appointed by the parent who had established the policies and procedures, he had a clear understanding of the joint venture's operating rules.

What role managers in parent companies play. Two crucial elements in determining the JVGM's autonomy are the personal style of managers from the parent companies and the amount of trust between people. In some joint ventures, the JVGM received calls on a periodic basis from managers in a parent company who wanted to make sure there were no surprises, while in other joint ventures the JVGM would be left alone (unless he asked for help) until the next board meeting.

6.4 HOW DO JVGMs RESPOND TO THOSE CHALLENGES?

Parent's *vs* joint venture's agenda

As JVGMs learn how to live and manage under double parenting, they tend to develop an agenda of their own which differs in

83

an important way from that of their parents. While managers from parent companies tend to decide on the joint venture's success based on how well the joint venture meets their own expectations, the JVGMs' judgement is based on the avoidance of bad relationships between the parties involved. In other words, managers in the parent companies tend to use indicators centred on the idea of achieving specific results, while JVGMs tend to use indicators centred on the idea of preventing bad relationships from developing. The following quotes capture the essence of the JVGMs' concern:

JVGM 1: 'If the joint venture is able to accomplish a desired result without too much "noise" it is a sign for future prosperous relationships.'

JVGM 2: 'For the joint venture to be successful I have to grow, to achieve the objectives set by the VP for Latin America, to maintain the leadership position we have in Mexico and to maintain a trust relationship between the Canadians and the Mexicans.'

JVGM 3: 'A good indication of the success of the joint venture is that one parent has been able to run the joint venture without interference from the other parent.'

In cases where the JVGM was a national of the host country, an important item on the agenda was the joint venture's contribution to the country's economic and social development. Nationalistic concerns appear to play a more important role in LDCs than in developed countries and were noted in joint ventures staffed with national top managers, be they appointed by the local or the multinational parent.

Parent's *vs* joint venture's interests

JVGMs tend to see their allegiance to the joint venture first and to the parents second. This applies to the vast majority of JVGMs interviewed, whether they come from one parent or not. When trying to resolve differences between the parents, they find that the joint venture's interests should be placed first and the parents' second.

Essentially JVGMs want to stay away from situations where one parent is perceived to win and the other to lose over a specific issue. If the JVGM tries to satisfy one parent more than the other, or if he is perceived to do so, sooner or later he is going to erode his credibility and jeopardise his working relationship with the partner who feels discriminated against.

When managers refer to a joint venture's interest, they implicitly conceptualise a criterion of what is good or bad for the joint venture. This criterion may be operationalised in a number of ways, depending on the manager, the joint venture, the circumstances in which it is used, etc. . . . For instance, one manager may decide that anything that improves the competitive posture of the joint venture is in its best interest. Another manager may decide that when facing a choice, the alternative which is expected to yield the highest profit has to be selected (assuming the joint venture is considered as a profit centre). Meanwhile, in one of the joint ventures which has been assigned a common set of objectives by its parents, a manager may decide that anything consistent with these objectives is in the best interest of the joint venture.

When the joint venture has been assigned a set of agreed-upon objectives, or is considered as a profit centre, by its two parents, it is easy to decide what is in the best interests of the joint venture. However, it is important to recognise that the joint venture's interests are a reflection of the parents' interests who define them: they are not independent. The separation between the joint venture's and a parent's interests occurs when the joint venture intends to carry out an activity which is consistent with its interests, as defined by its objectives, but which is contrary to a parent's interests. The typical example given by managers is when an MNE parent wants the joint venture to cut exports to foreign countries it can serve through a wholly-owned plant which has temporary overcapacity. In this case what is in the best interest of the joint venture is no longer in the best interest of the parent and conversely. Here the joint venture's position is well understood. It was originally defined (or at least agreed upon) by the parent itself.

In cases where the joint ventures does not have a specific set of objectives assigned, managers use the term 'joint venture's interest' to refer to undefined, non-explicit objectives that the joint venture would strive for were it an independent company (e.g. increase market share, maximise profits). In this sense the joint venture's interests are not necessarily a reflection of the parents' interests; they are simply a concept, an ideal, that managers feel useful as a means of settling a conflict between the two parents. They suggest that rather than seeing one partner win and the other lose over a specific issue, it might be better to see the joint venture win, even if in practice it is the same thing.

JVGMs' time orientation

The JVGMs' concern with preventing major clashes between and/or with the parents prompts them to be very prudent with the short-term impact of their decisions. As shown in Table 6.4, JVGMs from the ten Mexican joint ventures were short-term oriented while there was no such clear pattern for managers from the parent companies.

Three major factors were found to reinforce the JVGMs' short-term orientation:

In all cases at least one parent had a short-term orientation;
All JVGMs had a bonus tied to their joint venture's yearly results;
JVGMs frequently reported to the joint venture's board of directors and/or to the executive committee. For instance, 75 per cent of the boards of the Mexican joint ventures, met at least four times a year.

By holding JVGMs accountable through such close scrutiny, managers from parent companies inevitably trigger the JVGMs' short-term orientation. It does not mean that JVGMs are not concerned with the long-term health of the joint venture, but that when trade-offs have to be made, the short-term considerations carry the greatest weight in decision-making.

Not all JVGMs are alike, though, and it was observed that JVGMs with limited-term contracts (two-to-three years) had, not surprisingly, a shorter time orientation than JVGMs with longer-term contracts.

The JVGM as diplomat: facilitating commitment, trust and communication

Commitment is one of the key variables associated with the success of joint ventures — something the JVGM must be

Table 6.4: Time orientation of the partners involved in the joint ventures as reflected in their main criteria of success

JV	MNE parent	Local parent	JVGM
1)	Long-term: 'Optimise long-term shareholder's value through consistent real growth in earnings'	Short-term: Yearly growth rate Operating efficiency	Short-term: Sales and profit growth Profit margin on net sales
2)	Short-term: Profitability Growth	Long-term: Growth Joint venture as a tool to diversify parent's portfolio in hotel business	Short-term: Growth Profitability Successful middleman
3)	Long-term: Market share growth Search for opportunities in Mexico and Latin America	Short-term: Meet budgets Long-term: Develop growth potential	Short-term: Meet budgets 'No Noise'
4)	Short-term: Profits, growth, and quality of their own brand	Short-term: Operating results Long-term: Profits Growth Future prospects	Short-term: Avoid conflicts Achieve plan
5)	Short-term Return on net assets Dividends Business runs smoothly	Short-term: Profitability Contribution to Mexico Auto-financing	Short-term: Successful diplomat Long-term: Growth
6)	Long-term: Build long-term profit base Achieve strategic plan Identification of future growth opportunities	Short-term: Contribution to parent through transfer prices	Short-term: Monthly results Profits ROI

— *continued overleaf*

Table 6.4: — *continued*

JV MNE parent	Local parent	JVGM
7) Short-term: Achieve mission ROI Dividends	Long-term: Protection against erosion of money Fiscal benefits Mission (growth and exports)	Short-term: Maintain peace between partners Achieve plan (1 Year)
8) Short-term Achieve mission ROI Dividends Operating results Long-term: Successful implementation of strategy	Short-term: Short-term growth in sales and profit	Short-term: Operating results Long-term: Maintain leadership in Mexico Maintain trust between partners
9) Long-term: Volume growth Market share Vehicle to look for opportunities into Mexico	Short-term: Profitability Supplies from joint venture Information on market Long-term: Future growth	Short-term: Meet budgets Profitability
10) Short-term: Profits Long term: Re-establish parent reputation in Mexico	Short-term: Dividends Long-term: Build asset base in hotels and land for development	Short-term: Growth Profitability Successful middleman

Source: Schaan (1983), p. 210.

concerned with. There are four levels of commitment relevant to joint ventures: 1) commitment to international business; 2) commitment to joint venture success; 3) commitment to the particular joint venture; and 4) commitment to the particular venture partner. Table 4.2 provides a summary of the questionnaire responses, including those from the JVGMs.

In the high-performing joint ventures commitment in all four areas was high. Two of the four questions in every category were characteristic at a .10 level of significance or better. This suggests that commitment is indeed associated with success.

In aggregate the JVGMs felt that there was commitment from the MNE. At least one question from each level was rated as characteristic at the .20 level of significance or lower. Also, JVGMs felt that the increase in number of nationals employed was an important factor in joint-venture success. This relates directly to the importance of LDC contribution of knowledge of the local economy, politics and culture, and knowledge of local business practices. By having nationals employed as managers (and even as the JVGM), this knowledge is gained. This was also characteristic of the equity-holding general managers.

The JVGMs felt that the parents should have contingency plans available for assistance. This was true for the aggregate as well as for the equity-holding and non-equity-holding managers. This shows that the JVGMs would like to have visible support from their parents should the joint venture run into difficulties.

In aggregate the JVGMs felt that commitment to the particular joint venture (in terms of the joint-venture interests being placed first) was important. This reduces the conflicts of two sets of objectives or directions from the parents. Unfortunately, this was not characteristic from the MNE parents' point of view. The JVGMs must work to convince the parents of the importance of the joint venture's interests being placed first.

Also, in this category the willingness to visit and offer assistance by the parent was viewed as important by the JVGMs. This again shows the importance of parent assistance to the JVGM. Fortunately, this was also characteristic of the MNEs in high-performing ventures. This is a positive sign because those MNEs and JVGMs already have something vital in common — the willingness to visit and offer assistance.

For the non-equity JVGMs, the parents' willingness to commit resources was also very important. This is probably due to managerial confidence, i.e. if the joint venture needs something it is comforting to know that the parents would give it to the joint venture if necessary.

The JVGMs also viewed commitment to the particular venture partner as important. The willingness of the parent to hold regular meetings was deemed characteristic of the MNCs in high-performing ventures. These meetings encompassed an information session for the MNCs as well as feedback from them. In successful ventures there was this free flow of information. In

Reynolds' (1979) study of joint ventures in India, he similarly noted that:

> For the Indian, the choice of a partner is not so much the finding of an individual with whom he can feel compatible, since the individual partner-representative is likely to change every few years. It is more important to discover a company whose operating philosophy attracts individual managers who are likely to prove compatible.

The lack of parent commitment could also be seen in cases where there was no structure at headquarters to deal with the joint venture, or that there was structure, but a lack of resources allocated to it to operate efficiently. Successful control requires that a parent be committed to a joint venture and be prepared to allocate resources to exercise it.

The JVGM must also facilitate trust and open communications in the joint venture and between the parents. In turn, trust and communication will increase the parents' commitment toward the joint venture. Managers in successful parent companies have been found to spend time and money to maintain and develop a trust relationship with the JVGM or with their partners in order to increase the accuracy of information obtained through informal channels and discussions with managers from the joint venture or the local partner. Formal reports are not sufficient to determine what is really going on in the joint venture.

The JVGM is in a unique position to develop an understanding of the parents' idiosyncrasies with respect to verbal, non-verbal and written communications. He often has to serve as an interpreter by explaining the meaning of what is communicated, clarifying misunderstandings and teaching managers in the parents' organisations about their partners' codes and languages. The negative impact of poor communications on the partners' working relationship was also noted by Reynolds (1979).

Trust between the partners is a critical ingredient to the successful resolution of conflicts. This has been found to be particularly true for joint ventures in LDCs, where the quality of interpersonal relationships is a better predictor of successful conflict resolution than legal and contractual considerations. As a result, the JVGM needs to help the parents build a relationship where trust is an important component. Also, he must avoid situations which may jeopardise trust, because once lost it is extremely hard to rebuild. This also applies to his own relationship with the parents.

The trust-communication-commitment characteristics are truly integrated. By developing and maintaining an open communication system with the joint venture and with the partner, the parent is able to: 1) understand the joint venture's problems better and offer better solutions; 2) become aware of changes occurring in the joint venture business or in its partner's expectations; 3) keep in touch with its partner, hence showing commitment to the joint venture and contributing to a trust relationship.

The JVGM is often the centre of all the interaction between the two partners. By understanding the importance of open communication to a trusting relationship and how it achieves a higher level of commitment from the partners, the JVGM as diplomat can strive to open barriers that may be blocking this profitable cycle.

6.5 IMPLICATIONS

Implications for JVGMs

In order to cope with the political and interpersonal constraints of their job, JVGMs must show great sensitivity to the parent companies' differences in culture, management style and expectations. Being under the scrutiny of two or more parents, they have to reconcile the achievement of their personal and career objectives with the parents' objectives and with the unique strategic and operating imperatives of running a company in an LDC.

Since a distinct advantage of a joint ventures over a wholly-owned subsidiary is its access to the skills and resources of two parents, the JVGM has an implicit opportunity to use this advantage to his benefit. However, a potential limitation is that the need for parent support is generally crucial in the early stages of a joint venture, at a time when the JVGM has not yet built his networks with the parents.

Implications for managers in parent MNEs

Staffing. Managers in parent companies should be prepared to staff joint ventures in LDCs with local managers. This is all the more important when there is a tendency in MNEs to insist on providing management personnel to the joint venture. This is frequently the case of very large MNEs which tend to duplicate their managerial systems and processes in their foreign subsidiaries, or for companies which have little or no experience in LDCs and/or with joint ventures. In those two sets of circumstances the rationale for appointing expatriates is the belief that it reduces uncertainty by facilitating communications between the joint venture and the parent and by appointing as joint venture managers individuals whose managerial style and practices are known. However, such practice does not recognise that the skills and knowledge required to manage a joint venture successfully in an LDC are very different from those developed in managing wholly-owned subsidiaries and/or in developed countries.

For example, dealing with the local elites, business people, politicians and the local partner is a highly subtle exercise in diplomacy which may prove more important than the ability to run an operation effectively.

Developing a working relationship. In order to avoid surprises, to understand the operating context of the joint venture, to be able to ask the 'right' questions and to interpret the answers, managers in parent companies need to manage their relationships with the JVGM on the one hand and with the partner(s) on the other hand. In joint ventures, a relationship is something which is built over time, not something which is there when one needs it.

A good example is provided by the experience of the VP in a parent company involved in joint ventures around the world. The VP made it a point to spend 50 per cent of his time abroad with the local partners discussing business matters and 50 per cent fishing or visiting archaeological sites or museums. For him, developing a personal relationship was key for a healthy long-term business relationship.

Implications for researchers

Most research on joint ventures has emphasised issues from the parents' perspective and very little attention has been paid to the JVGM. This chapter presents some of the dimensions which define the JVGM's strategic and operating decision-making context. However, this area needs to be conceptually strengthened.

Future research might examine joint ventures operating in developed countries and compare the role of the JVGM with that of the general managers in wholly-owned subsidiaries. Useful designs to research such topics could control for parent company effect by comparing a number of subsidiaries of one multinational firm, or could focus on cross-national comparisons.

6.6 CONCLUSION

Ambiguity is inherent to the practice of management. An important element in the successful performance of general management activities is the ability to find one's way in a complex web of people, structures, roles and so forth. This is also true for general managers of joint ventures operating in LDCs. Here the complexity is heightened by the double parenting, the geographical as well as the cultural 'distance', and the general infrastructure in which the joint venture operates. In that sense, a major challenge facing JVGMs in LDCs is that in addition to being 'good' general managers, they also have to be good diplomats, able to operate constantly within two — or more — frames of reference and sets of values, and to manage the idiosyncrasies of their parents with success.

NOTE

*This chapter was co-authored by Jean-Louis Schaan. An earlier version was published in Contractor and Lorange (1987) and also appears as University of Ottawa Working Paper 87-4. The authors wish to acknowledge the research assistance of Ms Itrath Qizilbash.

7

Equity Joint Ventures and the Theory of the Multinational Enterprise*

Limited consideration has been given to the rationale for equity joint ventures in the theory of the multinational enterprise. While recent theoretical contributions utilising the internalisation approach have significantly advanced our understanding of MNEs (Buckley and Casson, 1976; Casson, 1979, 1982; Rugman, 1979), the theory offers only partial explanations of the ownership preferences of MNEs for other than wholly-owned subsidiaries (Davidson and McFetridge, 1985; Teece, 1983; Thorelli, 1986; Horstmann and Markusen, 1986; Wells, 1973). The purpose of this chapter is to extend the internalisation approach further by providing an economic rationale for joint ventures within the framework provided by the transactions cost paradigm. When examining their economic rationale it is important to distinguish between equity- and contractually-based joint ventures. In the case of the former, the explicit intention of the partners is to manage the JV as a going-concern over the long term. Contractual JVs, however, are established for a fixed time period with the explicit intention of the partners at the outset to dissolve the relationship at a specified date (for a discussion of contractual joint ventures, see Wright, 1981, p. 500). In this chapter we are concerned only with equity JVs.

In the next section, the main features of internalisation theory are reviewed. This is followed by a discussion of how the theory can be extended to joint ventures using the transactions cost paradigm developed by Williamson (1975). In the final section empirical evidence supporting some of the predictions of this expanded notion of internalisation theory will be examined.

7.1 THE THEORY OF INTERNALISATION

Internalisation theory was developed to provide an economic rationale for the existence of MNEs. By definition these firms establish local operations as a means of serving a foreign market rather than engaging in arm's-length transactions with market intermediaries. The theory posits that due to the transaction costs which must be borne as a result of conducting business in imperfect markets, it is more efficient (less expensive) for the firm to use internal structures rather than market intermediaries to serve a foreign market. According to Williamson's (1975) reasoning these market imperfections arise from two environmental conditions: uncertainty and a small number of market agents. When these conditions coexist with two sets of human factors, opportunism and bounded rationality, he argues that the costs of writing, executing and enforcing arm's-length complex contingent claims contracts with market intermediaries are greater than the costs of internalising the market.[1] In other words, a firm facing a complex, unpredictable business environment and having a few potential channel members to utilise would be more profitable performing the distribution function itself when there was a strong likelihood market agents would try to take advantage of the firm's lack of complete knowledge and the firm was unable to specify all possible future transaction contingencies.

Researchers in international business have been very successful in providing an economic rationale for the establishment of an MNE as a response to imperfect markets, utilising transactions cost logic (Buckley and Casson, 1976; Caves, 1982; Dunning, 1981; Hennart, 1982; Rugman, 1981; Teece, 1981, 1983). In extending this logic to international markets they have found it useful to distinguish between strategies of vertical integration and horizontal diversification since the nature of market failures is different in each situation. The economic reasoning supporting the internalisation of markets in the case of vertical integration is concerned with the failure of markets in intermediate goods. In the case of horizontal diversification, the concern is with the failure of markets in intangible assets for such things as management know-how, trade name or proprietory technology. Although the elegance and comprehensiveness of transactions cost reasoning has provided the internalisation approach with a powerful logic (Rugman, 1981, 1985), it is still deficient in some respects as a general theory of the MNE. The major limitation is that the theory in its current form focuses primarily on one mode of hierarchy or organisation. It therefore provides the firm with only one fully developed solution to the problem of imperfect international markets — the establishment of a wholly-owned subsidiary (WOS). Yet, both conceptually and practically, there are a number of other modes which firms can and do adopt to deal with imperfections in international markets including licensing, management contracts, subcontracting, joint-ventures and consortia. Moreover, firms often employ several different modes simultaneously in addressing the needs of a particular foreign market (Contractor, 1985; Davidson and McFetridge, 1985). Thus, for the internalisation approach to be regarded as a general theory of the MNE it will have to provide an economic rationale for these other modes (Hennart, 1985) and specify the conditions under which each would provide efficiency gains over WOSs and the market. The objective of this chapter is to provide a rationale for equity JVs within the internalisation framework.

7.2 JOINT VENTURES AND INTERNALISATION THEORY

In order to justify the utilisation of international JVs within the internalisation framework two necessary conditions must be shown to exist: the firm possesses a rent-yielding asset which would allow it to be competitive in a foreign market; and joint-venture arrangements are superior to other means for appropriating rents from the sale of this asset in the foreign market (Teece, 1983). A detailed explanation for the possession of a sustainable competitive advantage regardless of the means employed for exploiting it in international markets has already been provided by Dunning and Rugman (1985). Likewise, the conditions within which JVs provide a superior means of exploiting these assets for firms pursuing international vertical integration has been extensively considered by Stuckey (1983) using the transaction cost paradigm. However, a similarly extensive consideration of JVs in the context of international horizontal diversification strategies is currently lacking in the literature. Thus the focus of this chapter will be on the latter case.

Following Teece (1983) we would argue that the attractiveness of joint ventures is a function of both the revenue-enhancing and cost-reducing opportunities they provide the MNE. However, according to internalisation theory in its present formulation, firms would have a strong economic incentive always to avoid joint-venture arrangements since these are regarded as being inferior to WOSs in allowing the firm to maximise the returns available on its ownership-specific advantages (Caves, 1982; Rugman, 1983; Killing, 1983; Poynter, 1985; Harrigan, 1985). The value of the foreign local partners' assets would apparently be insufficient in any conceivable situation to offset the strategic risks and transactions costs faced by the MNE in exploiting its ownership-specific assets. Yet this solution to the problem of imperfect markets assumes that management has the ability to organise an internal market and that a joint venture cannot be structured in such a way as to maintain both the bargaining and maladaption costs inherent in such arrangements at acceptable levels. Thus, in its current state of development, internalisation theory focuses primarily on the situation where WOS and arm's-length transactions are the only alternatives available to deal with Williamson's (1975) market-disabling factors of opportunism, bounded rationality, uncertainty and small numbers.

However, we would suggest that JVs which conform to certain preconditions and structural arrangements can actually provide a better solution to the problems of opportunism, small numbers dilemma and uncertainty in the face of bounded rationality than wholly-owned subsidiaries. Although there would be costs associated with writing, executing and enforcing pricing agreements and use restrictions regarding the transfer of the MNE's intangible assets, these will be more than offset by the enhanced revenue potential of its assets as a result of forming a JV. As well, rents can exceed those available through wholly-owned subsidiaries due to the the potential synergistic effects of combining the MNE's assets with those of the local partner. The following section will identify the conditions under which we feel market failure due to opportunism, the small numbers dilemma and uncertainty can be efficiently addressed through joint-venture arrangements. Most of the following illustrations and examples of how market failure can be efficiently addressed are drawn from Beamish (1984), and discussed in detail in the section on empirical evidence.

One of the most significant transactional contingencies faced by MNEs considering a joint venture would apparently be provoked by the problem of opportunism. Yet even Williamson (1975, 1983) allows that opportunistic behaviour is not necessarily an inevitable aspect of inter-firm behaviour although he suspects such situations would be uncommon. We would suggest that in situations where a joint venture is established in a spirit of mutual trust and commitment to its long-term commercial success, opportunistic behaviour is unlikely to emerge. This is similar to the concept of mutual forbearance (Buckley and Casson, 1987), where agents on a reciprocal basis, deliberately pass up short-term advantages. With a foundation of trust the partner, and particularly the MNE, would be more willing to exercise the tolerance and perseverance necessary to see the joint venture through its difficult times. Problems could be effectively dealt with by the MNE without damaging the long-run viability and efficiency of the joint venture arrangement. In these circumstances the effective management of opportunism would depend far more on managerial perspicacity and persistence than on company lawyers masterminding complete contingent claims contracts.[2] Furthermore, if these positive attitudes are reinforced with supporting inter-organisational linkages such as mechanisms for the division of profits, joint decision-making processes and reward and control systems, the incentives to engage in self-seeking pre-emptive behaviour could be minimised (Williamson, 1983). Under such circumstances, then, opportunism is not likely to obtain as the parties would be able to pursue their own self interest without a need to resort to guile. They could negotiate a shared perception of the relative value of their respective contributions over time and establish a mutually acceptable division of profits in a vigorous yet open fashion (Berg and Friedman, 1980). Their attention could be directed toward long-term joint profit maximisation since there would be no need to make pre-emptive claims on profit streams. Consequently the partners could take the long view for investment purposes while simultaneously adjusting to changing market circumstances in an adaptive sequential manner.

A small numbers situation, particularly when combined with opportunism, would normally result in serious transactional difficulties for the firm (Williamson, 1975). In the case of joint ventures, even if initially there are several local firms from which to select a suitable partner, a small numbers condition could obtain if the firm wished to change the terms of the agreement at a later date and seek a new partner. Having some experience with the MNE, the initial local partner will clearly enjoy cost advantages over firms not selected at the outset. The option of switching partners is, therefore, not optimal for the MNE. However, in the absence of local partner opportunism, this small numbers situation could present much less serious transactional difficulties than normally might be expected. Moreover, by establishing those inter-organisational linkages referred to earlier, it is possible to manage many of the types of difficulties associated with exchange between bilateral monopolists regarding individual or joint maximisation of profits (Contractor, 1985). There will be much less incentive to secure gains by strategic posturing and the interests of the joint venture can be promoted. Thus, under certain conditions, the small numbers dilemma can be effectively dealt with in a joint venture.

The problem of uncertainty can also be handled efficiently within some international joint ventures. In the absence of opportunism and small numbers disabilities there are strong incentives for the parties to pool their respective resources. By doing so it is possible for the MNE to economise on the information requirements of foreign investment (Caves, 1982; Beamish, 1984; Rugman, 1985). The MNE can provide firm-specific knowledge regarding technology, management and capital markets while the local partner can provide location-specific knowledge regarding host country markets, infrastructure and political trends. By pooling and sharing information through the mechanism of a joint venture the MNE is able to reduce uncertainty at a lower long-term average cost than through pure hierarchical or market approaches. Because the parties would have little incentive to behave opportunistically the derivative condition of information impactedness due to uncertainty and opportunism would not arise. Although bounded rationality would continue to be a problem, a pure hierarchical mode of transacting would not represent a superior solution to this problem alone. The low costs associated with opportunism, small numbers, uncertainty and information impactedness in joint ventures under the conditions specified above would render this mode of transacting the most efficient means of serving a foreign market.

Theoretically, although they have advantages over the market and wholly-owned subsidiaries in certain circumstances, there are limits to the relative efficiency gains provided by joint ventures. First, they can suffer from the same goal distortions as hierarchies. The MNE can become biased towards the maintenance of its initial arrangements with the joint-venture partner without considering the long-term profit or cost implications. However, several approaches to ensuring that profitability goals are not subordinated to other considerations or that the joint-venture mode of transaction is not uncritically preserved can be taken. For instance, profitability goals can be maintained by giving the general manager an equity position in the joint venture. This provides a strong incentive for him to ensure that profits are earned in the joint venture itself and are not unequally siphoned to one partner over the other. Mechanisms can also be established which prevent either partner having total control over distribution or final selling price. Clearly, the lower the price to the distributor, the greater the profit that the distributing partner does not have to share. As well, management fees (usually paid to the MNE) can be tied to the productivity/profitability of the joint venture and the length of management contracts can be held to a relatively short time period. Not tying the joint ventures to a single source of supply, particularly if it is one of the partners, can help ensure that procurement biases are minimised. Finally, a conscious effort can be made to ensure that the total income derived from the joint venture by each partner, even if the mechanisms for doing so differ, are approximately equal. Contractor (1985) has noted that many overseas ventures are being formed as a mix of direct investment, licensing and trade. He suggests that the joint venture partner may be compensated by a package involving some return on equity investments, royalties, technical service and management fees, and/or margins on components or finished product traded with the joint venture. Both Schaan (1983) and Beamish (1984) found evidence of such approaches. In both their LDC-based samples, virtually none of the foreign partners relied solely on dividends for compensation. In fact, on average, they had nearly two additional sources. In contrast, about one-third of the local partners relied solely on dividends, with the balance having one other source of income.

Ensuring the joint venture arrangement is not uncritically maintained requires explicit recognition by both parties that: a partner may resort to guile at some point (even if this was absent in his behaviour at the outset, if the absolute number of locally available managers increases, the need for a foreign partner and his ability to supply management resources may be reduced);

and while the foreign partner may possess the requisite knowledge about the local economy, politics and culture at the outset he may not continue to put forth the effort necessary to maintain this knowledge. Commitment to the success of joint ventures often varies over time. From the MNE's perspective the level of ongoing commitment may be a function of who in the firm helped set up the joint venture and his current status with the company (Aharoni, 1966; Beamish, 1984).

The risk of leakage of proprietary knowledge also serves to limit the efficiency gains available through joint-venture arrangements. Leakage can occur in one of two major ways: a local employee may decide to resign and use the knowledge acquired in the joint venture to establish a competing firm (type 1); or the local partner may decide to dissolve the arrangement and use the knowledge gained through the joint venture as a basis for continuing to serve the local (and possibly a foreign) market through his own organisation (type 2). Type 1 leakages are especially hard to prevent particularly if the employee concerned recognises the personal trade-offs involved and is willing to live with some limitations such as being forced to serve a single market. Type 2 leakages are often easier to control because the negative consequences for the local partner can be quite significant. Pirating the MNE's existing technology will normally mean that the local partner loses access to export markets, ongoing technological developments, trademarks, marketing skills and possibly specialised raw materials. Moreover depending on how the original agreement was structured, this pirating of technology might even be construed as a form of industrial espionage. Presumably the threat of lawsuits would act as a disincentive. Certainly there is, however, a dilution of complete control with industrial espionage (Buckley, 1985: 46). Leakage, therefore, is a problem in joint ventures and its costs do serve to limit the efficiency gains joint ventures offer markets and hierarchies (Parry, 1985; Rugman, 1985).

Notwithstanding the potential for technology leakage, what seems often to be overlooked by management in the overall economic evaluation of joint ventures is that even though the start-up costs of wholly-owned subsidiaries may be substantially lower, the long-term average costs may be much higher than joint ventures due to the very significant cost associated with independent efforts to overcome a lack of knowledge about the local economy, politics and culture.

101

7.3 EMPIRICAL EVIDENCE

This section reviews recent joint venture studies by Beamish, Wells (1983) and Stuckey (1983) as they related to internalisation theory. Beamish (1984) was reviewed in the earlier chapters. Beamish incorporates supporting evidence from other joint-venture researchers, including Artisien and Buckley (1985), Schaan (1983), Killing (1983), Janger (1980) and Tomlinson (1970) and was the source of many of the previously cited examples.

Caves (1982) provides two positive reasons — both of which are consistent with the observations and transactions approach in this study — that cause MNEs to seek out joint ventures. The first of these is the MNE's lack of some capacity or competence needed to make the investment succeed. An obvious case is the MNE diversifying geographically and lacking in managerial know-how for competing in the new market. Another reason lies in the MNE's need for specific resources possessed by local joint-venture partners. These needs include knowledge about local marketing or other environmental conditions. In fact, Stopford and Wells (1972) observe that the major contribution to the MNE of local partners at the time of formation of joint ventures is local knowledge. Joint ventures economise on the information requirements of foreign investment and are thus likely to appeal when these information requirements are most burdensome. Caves adds that joint ventures seem to be prevalent as MNEs proceed towards more unfamiliar host countries, citing Saham's (1980: 150–1) finding that joint ventures are uncommon in culturally familiar LDC settings.

In Chapter 2 we observed that the characteristics of joint ventures in less developed countries differed from those in developed countries. Differences were noted in stability,[3] autonomy, ownership, reasons for creating the venture, and management control. This issue of control has been particularly important in joint-venture research. From his joint-venture research in developed countries Killing (1983), like Kolde (1974), concluded that one partner should assume dominant control and operate the venture as if it were a wholly-owned subsidiary. Concluding that control of the joint venture should not be shared, Killing implies that wholly-owned subsidiaries may be more appropriate than joint ventures in the developed countries. That these LDC observations differ from those in developed countries is not inconsistent with the earlier hypothesis. Killing's results suggest that there are relatively lower requirements for adaptation and information for the MNE when it invests in other developed (versus developing) countries. In such a case, the MNE's advantage — firm-specific knowledge of production/marketing — is sufficient.[4]

Unlike Killing, Janger (1980) found in his study of joint ventures in developed and developing countries that one control structure could not be identified as more successful than the others. Tomlinson's (1970) study of joint ventures lead him to conclude that the MNEs should not insist on dominant control over the major managerial decisions in joint ventures located in LDCs. He felt that the sharing of responsibility with local associates would lead to a greater contribution from them and, in turn, to a greater return on investment. The control questionnaire developed by Killing for use with developed country joint ventures was administered by Beamish (1984) to the MNE partners in the core ventures in his LDC sample. There was a significant relationship between unsatisfactory performance and overall foreign-dominant control, and between satisfactory performance and shared or local-dominant control. In fact, the MNE partners in the unsuccessful ventures preferred to operate without a partner as much as possible. Unlike the MNE partners in the successful ventures, they were unwilling to share control in exchange for access to local managers and their local knowledge. In the successful shared-control ventures, both partners had placed significant value on the others' contributions over time. The perception of a mutual long-term need between the partners reduced the propensity to act opportunistically.

As well, Artisien and Buckley (1985: Table 12) found that where the MNE's motive for preferring a joint venture (over other forms of trade and industrial cooperation with Yugoslav enterprises) was 'to achieve greater participation in decision-making', the mean success rating for the JV was 'very successful'. This correlation between shared decision-making control and joint-venture success is similar to that observed in LDCs. In both LDCs and socialist market economies, such as Yugoslavia (see also Cory, 1982), MNEs from developed countries may well be confronted with higher adaptation and information requirements than they are accustomed, thus reinforcing the appropriateness of joint ventures.

7.4 LOCAL KNOWLEDGE AND PERFORMANCE

Beamish's (1984) examination of the importance attached by the MNE to the local partner's ownership-specific assets also provided data regarding the determinants of joint-venture success. As discussed in Chapter 3, interviewees were asked to assess the importance of the partner's contribution to the venture of 16 different items. The pattern of results observed when the importance of the local-partner contributions to the MNE were compared in the successful and unsuccessful ventures was consistent with the predictions of internalisation theory. Differences in the value attached to the importance of the local partner's contribution were observed between the successful and unsuccessful ventures in terms of human resource needs, government/political needs and knowledge needs. Significantly, the MNE partners in the successful ventures deemed important their local partner's contributions of general managers, functional managers, general knowledge of the local economy, politics and culture, and knowledge of current business practice. Not only was none of these local-partner contributions important to the MNE partners in the unsuccessful ventures, but these MNE partners went so far as to class the local partner's contribution of general and functional managers as unimportant. Of significance here is the association between success and obtaining access to local knowledge, and the association between lack of success and not attaching importance to this local-partner contribution. In transaction-cost terms, successful partnerships economised on the information requirements of foreign investment and reduced uncertainty by pooling their resources.

The only areas in which the MNE partner in the unsuccessful ventures felt their local partners made important contributions were in the areas of satisfying existing or forecast government requirements for local ownership. In such cases, any local partner would suffice since it was only access to the local partner's nationality (as opposed to knowledge) that was desired. With any national sufficing as a partner, there would obviously be no small numbers constraint. Yet, when a partner was chosen simply for his nationality, poor performance resulted. Although the MNE imposes the small numbers condition on itself by choosing a partner who can contribute knowledge, such a condition does not necessarily become a dilemma. As discussed earlier, if the likelihood of opportunistic behaviour has already been reduced (as it is here where each partner acknowledges the significant contribution(s) of the other), small numbers transactional difficulties are also lower.

As noted in Chapter 4, where joint ventures are established in a spirit of mutual trust and commitment to long-term success, opportunism was believed much less likely to emerge. To measure commitment and its relationship to joint-venture performance, the general managers of twelve JVs were asked to complete a questionnaire, the purpose of which was to assess how characteristic a total of 16 statements were of the foreign (MNE) parent-company's attitudes and activities *vis-à-vis* joint ventures and/or the particular joint venture.

Two of the characteristic statements in the high-performing ventures were: management from the parent company is quite willing to visit regularly and offer assistance to the joint venture, and we try to ensure that through regular meetings, each partner knows what to expect from the joint venture. These statements in particular were consistent with a sense of commitment — the antithesis of opportunism.

Not surprisingly, there was a strong correlation between the commitment results and several other constructs — specifically need and control. Those firms exhibiting a willingness to be flexible and undertake a particular activity while controlling their opportunistic behaviour (commitment) were likely to be the same firms favouring a sharing of decision-making (control) and looking for greater contributions (need) from their partners.

Observations from joint-venture studies in slightly different contexts are reported in this section; 90 per cent of the manufacturing subsidiaries established by third world multinationals in Wells' (1983) recent study were joint ventures. None of this investment took place in other developing countries. Wells noted that the competitive advantage which the third world investors could offer derived from technologies enabling them to manufacture at low cost. These technologies involved small-scale flexible plants and considerable use of local inputs. Due to a lack of data about the contributions which a local partner could make to a developing country foreign investor, Wells speculated that the same contributions important to developed-country investors would exist. Consequently, third world MNEs are considered similar to the MNEs from the developed countries in Beamish's (1984) study, in that presumably they could benefit equally well from the local market knowledge their partners could provide.

105

Wells expects the life cycles of many manufacturing subsidiaries of developing country firms to be short because the MNE is not able to provide a sustainable competitive advantage. While the MNE may continue to require knowledge of the local economy, politics and culture from the local partner, the local partner will be able to copy the MNE's contribution much faster. Third world MNEs were found to be rarely building trade names, undertaking research and development, or concentrating their efforts on activities from which they could build a sustainable advantage. While the third world MNEs did seem to be benefiting from what we have called type-2 leakages of proprietary technology, these benefits were generally not long term. The benefits of what Wells calls partial internalisation would seem to be shorter for third world MNEs than for the MNEs from developed countries in Beamish's study (1984).

Stuckey's (1983) research indicated that vertically integrated firms in the aluminium industry shared one of the motivations for forming joint ventures with horizontally integrated firms. He found a primary reason for creating joint ventures was because technical know-how and management expertise (intangible assets) are not easily exchanged via markets to the satisfaction of both suppliers and buyers. Stuckey feels the need for 'nation-specific' knowledge typically arises when an established firm decides to invest in a country where they have had limited previous experience. Local firms or groups possess specialised information on the country's economy, politics, culture and so on, information that is costly and time consuming for the multinational enterprise to gather. This information is more accessible and is synthesised and used more efficiently within the relatively cooperative atmosphere of a joint venture, enabling the MNE to deal better with uncertainty. In summary, Stuckey feels the joint venture firm can be more efficient because it allows some of the economically important relationships between otherwise separate partners to be internalised by one organisation (1983: 152).

Cory (1982), in his research on industrial cooperation agreements and joint ventures between Yugoslav enterprises and Western MNEs, provides empirical support that such intermediate mechanisms can, and occasionally do, represent viable intermediate, or what he calls quasi-internalised mechanisms, for resource allocation. As in this chapter, Cory (1982: 167) notes that joint venture arrangements can incorporate the essential elements of internalised relationships between the partners.

7.5 CONCLUSIONS

Internalisation theory, as it is presently formulated, provides limited consideration of the efficiency and revenue gains available through joint-venture arrangements. Although the notion that local firms may have resources which could be useful is not precluded, the theory posits that it would be less expensive for the MNE to develop these resources internally than to acquire them by establishing a joint venture. Due to transactions disabilities which are assumed to be inherent in such inter-firm arrangements, whatever the MNE might gain in terms of knowledge of the local market, customs, business practices, contacts and government, it would apparently lose because of the costs associated with protecting its firm-specific assets from exploitation by the local partner. Thus, according to internalisation theory, a rational profit-maximising MNE would tend to use wholly-owned subsidiaries. Yet this view presupposes that none of Williamson's (1975) transactional disabilities — opportunism, bounded rationality, uncertainty and small numbers condition can be dealt efficiently within a JV. By demonstrating this assumption need not hold in all circumstances we have attempted to provide a theoretical justification for joint ventures within the context of internalisation theory. Under particular arrangements the potential threats posed by opportunism, a small numbers condition and uncertainty can be reduced to a point where JVs become a more efficient means of dealing with environmental uncertainty and maximising the profit potential of the MNE's firm-specific assets, even in the face of bounded rationality.

Previous research on joint-venture performance reviewed in this chapter provides support for our view. Not all joint ventures are necessarily unstable or unprofitable arrangements for MNEs. Beamish (1984) has shown that not only are there clearly discernible differences in the characteristics of successful and unsuccessful joint ventures but also that these characteristics are consistent with the predictions of internalisation theory in its expanded form. Forming a joint venture in an LDC is not without its cost. Nevertheless, the research we have conducted and

107

reviewed has shown that joint ventures were more efficient than wholly-owned subsidiaries for the MNE in LDC markets under certain circumstances and are consistent with Dunning's (1981) rationale for the appropriateness of joint ventures in place of wholly-owned subsidiaries.

Further research is required to determine if one element of local knowledge — economic, political or cultural — is more significant than others to MNEs. Also, because only an LDC-based sample of joint ventures was used, further research is required to determine whether the theory is applicable in joint ventures between partners from two developed countries with significantly different cultures, and to joint ventures between partners from two planned economies.

There are a wide range of international industrial cooperation modes now being studied in the context of internalisation. This chapter provides an expanded role for one of these modes — joint ventures — in the theory of the multinational enterprise.

NOTES

*This chapter was co-authored by John C. Banks. An earlier version appeared in the *Journal of International Business Studies* and is reproduced with permission.

1. Although the terminology developed by Williamson (1975) can be turgid for the uninitiated, it contains a precision which we find useful for our present purposes. The definitions of these terms are as follows: uncertainty/complexity — an environmental condition where specification of the full decision tree is infeasible; small numbers — an environmental condition where only one or two market agents are available to perform the required tasks; opportunism — a human condition manifested by the strategic manipulation of information or the misrepresentation of intentions including self-interest seeking behaviour with guile; bounded rationality — a human condition characterised by a limited capacity in terms of knowledge, foresight and skill which places limits on the individual's ability to comprehend complexity; information impactedness — a derivative condition in which the underlying circumstances relevant to the transaction, or related set of transactions, are known to one or more parties but cannot be costlessly discerned or displayed for others.

2. In game situations analogous to MNE-local-firm joint ventures, it has been shown that the development of cooperation can be promoted by a non-myopic player. By adopting a strategy based on trust and foresight the MNE could therefore convey its commitment to the joint venture and teach the local partner to respond in a cooperative fashion (Axelrod, 1984; Brams and Kilgour, 1985).

3. In a recent study of joint ventures in the USA, Kogut (1987) found an instability rate as high as that which until now was only observed in LDCs. Included in his sample were ventures which had been in operation less than three years.

4. Although not the focus of this chapter, it may be that internalisation theory can be reconciled to the view that joint ventures by MNEs are less appropriate in developed countries than in LDCs.

8

Investing in China via Joint Ventures

8.1 INTRODUCTION

The 1979 Joint Venture Law of the People's Republic of China (PRC) served as an increasingly powerful magnet for foreign investment over the past eight years. During the period 1979–84 the number of joint ventures (JVs) established increased almost exponentially, rising to 640 in 1984 alone.

Interest in China has evolved from a period of caution in the early 1980s, to the present explosion of involvement, what Pye (1986) has called the Westchester County Syndrome. This syndrome has resulted in US and other Western CEOs rushing to China to 'score points at their country clubs or among business associates'. This interest in China has been as much a rational interest in a newly opening large market as it has been an almost irrational desire to get in line for a retailer's big sale — even when you aren't sure what is being offered for sale.

In our view, the last part of the 1980s will be characterised by a more sober view of what the stakes are for doing business in China. By presenting and analysing *disaggregated* data on 840 joint ventures in China, it is possible for the foreign company contemplating investment to separate some of the fact from fiction about this market.

In this chapter we have taken the descriptions of 840 joint ventures from the *China Investment Guide* (1985, 1986), compiled them into a computerised data base and statistically analysed them using a frequencies programme. These are presented in nine tables. These hard data on China — of which there is a dearth — has then been combined in the analysis with the authors' personal experience doing business in China.

8.2   NEED FOR 'HARD' DATA ON CHINA

Although there has been a steady supply of anecdotal information on China, many of the 'insights' offered by observers have been based on very small samples. Furthermore, as Walls (1986) notes, 'They tell more about the observer than about the observed, since most observers tend to see what they expect to see, need to see or want to see.' One implication of having some larger-sample history regarding JVs in China is that it should be now possible for foreign investors to make a more informed decision about entering into a JV in that country. Until recently, most of the information on JVs in China was of three types. The first type was anecdotal (i.e. 'war stories' from the front-line market entrants) and was from the perspective of the foreign firms. The second type — from the Chinese perspective first but foreign perspective subsequently — was technical (i.e. the 118 articles of the 1983 'Regulations for the Implementation of the Law of the People's Republic of China on Joint Ventures Using Chinese and Foreign Investment'). This technical type of writing from China in turn spawned a large amount of legal and accounting interpretation within each foreign country contemplating investment. (Not surprisingly, due to on-going changes in the legal and accounting area in China, much of the published foreign country interpretation is out of date before it is even published.) The third type of information — from the Chinese perspective — was promotional. As China's modernisation programme evolved and gained momentum, there has been no reluctance to advertise the number of JVs signed, the billions of investment dollars committed, the regulatory changes designed to improve conditions and so forth.

This promotional material, because it was typically presented in aggregate form, has contributed to the recent bandwaggon effect for investment in China.

8.3   ANALYSIS

When foreign companies are thinking about where to invest in China, they are typically pointed in the direction of the four special economic zones, in major municipalities such as Beijing, Shanghai, Guangzhou or Tianjin or in the 14 coastal cities. As Table 8.1 indicates, most investment has taken place in these areas.

Table 8.1: Region of investment in China

	Frequency	%
Special economic zones	325	38.7
Economic and technical development zones		
(14 coastal cities)	226	26.9
Beijing	42	5.0
Other regions of China	247	29.4
Total	840	100.0

While focus on these areas does dramatically reduce the search time for where to locate investment, frustration remains. Due to a lack of coordination between regions, for most projects it is still necessary to approach officials in *each* province, major municipality, coastal city or special economic zone (SEZ) to determine if demand exists.

The implication of this should not be lost on firms considering investment in China. Particularly with regard to smaller investments — for which a higher degree of decentralised decision-making power exists in China — foreign firms must recognise that there may be literally dozens of regions/groups that can be approached. One strategy successfully employed by foreign firms wondering if there is a need in China for the technology they possess has been to write/telex each group several months before visiting the country. This may seem unnecessarily redundant. However, China, like most developing countries, does not possess sufficiently advanced management information systems. For example, it has nothing like the system of the Hong Kong Trade Development Council's trade enquiry data bank, which contains information on more than 18,000 local manufacturers, exporters and importers and a file or more than 80,000 overseas importers (*South China Morning Post*, 1985).

When the aggregate statistics about the thousand of JVs which have been signed are presented, what is not made clear who is who the partners typically are, and in which industry the investment occurs. Up to 1984, over three-quarters of the JVs in China were with partners from Hong Kong (Table 8.2). This provides support for Hong Kong's oft-voiced view that it is the 'gateway' to China.

Table 8.2: Source of JV investment in China

	Frequency	%
Hong Kong and Macao	658	78.3
USA	59	7.0
Japan	55	6.5
Europe	31	3.7
South East Asia	30	3.6
Australia and New Zealand	7	.8
Total	840	100.0

The existence of Hong Kong-based firms as either competitor or conduit, has sometimes gone unnoticed by European and other Western firms. In particular, a Hong Kong firm as conduit can be a reasonable approach to the Chinese market. For example, a European firm with unique and desirable technology may wish to enter the Chinese market but lack the particular managerial resources or cultural sensitivities to do so quickly. It can however provide the technology to a Hong Kong firm (either through a licence or joint venture), which in turn will establish a joint venture in China. The benefits of the third party's (Hong Kong) contribution of management and Chinese market cultural knowledge can exceed the cost of sharing any profits with a third group.

Most of the JVs which have been established have been in the manufacturing sector (Table 8.3). The second largest area of investment has been in accommodation. In particular, tourism has been an important source of foreign exchange in the service sector.

While the mega-projects such as Three Gorges hydro development and AMC auto assembly receive the headlines, most of the investments — no matter where the source — involved a total investment of less than $5 million (Table 8.4). In only about 5% of cases (Table 8.5) did the foreign partner's contribution exceed $5 million. For most multinationals this means it is possible to limit investment to manageable levels. A further implication, as

113

alluded to earlier, is that with decentralised decision-making for investments under $5.0 million, this provides further support for the need for foreign firms to investigate vigorously across China the potential for joint venturing.

Table 8.3: Industry divisions for JV investments in China, by SIC code

	Frequency	%
A) Agriculture and related services	5	.7
B) Fishing and trapping	10	1.5
C) Mining	19	2.8
E) Manufacturing	408	59.9
F) Construction	40	5.9
G) Transportation and services	20	2.9
I) Wholesale trade	26	3.8
J) Retail trade	2	.3
K Finance and insurance	2	.3
L) Real estate	3	.4
M) Business services	23	3.4
O) Educational services	1	.1
Q) Accommodation	66	9.7
R) Other	56	8.2
Total	681	100.0

Table 8.4: Total investment

	Hong Kong and Macao	USA	Japan	Europe	Other	Total	
Under $5m	565	42	45	23	28	703	(85.6%)
$5–10m	38	8	6	4	3	59	(7.2%)
$10–50m	31	5	3	3	6	48	(5.9%)
Over $50m	5	4	1	1	0	11	(1.4%)
Total	639	59	55	31	37	821	(100.0%)

Table 8.5: Foreign partner equity contribution

	Frequency	%
Under $5m	791	94.2
$5–10m	22	2.6
$10–50m	25	3.0
Over $50m	2	.2
Total	840	100.0

INVESTING IN CHINA VIA JOINT VENTURES

One consideration which has received much attention is the requirement to use a joint venture as opposed to wholly-owned subsidiary. China has made much of the fact that firms are no longer required to use the joint venture organisation form, but that if they choose to use it, majority foreign ownership is permitted. While this is certainly true, in practice the foreign firm had majority ownership in fewer than ten per cent of the JVs formed (Table 8.6). This frequent use of a minority-equity position by the foreign partner is consistent with joint ventures in market-economy developing countries as well (Chapter 2).

Table 8.6: Foreign equity percentage

5–24%	=	24
25%	=	88
26–48%	=	313
49%	=	60
50%	=	247
51–99%	=	73
		805

The most frequently observed foreign equity percentage was 50 per cent (Table 8.7). Use of equal ownership is consistent with the underlying Chinese desire for mutual benefit. Equal ownership does not necessarily require equal control over all decisions within the joint venture. Decision-making may be shared between the partners, or split. For example, in the Fujian-Hitachi Television Ltd joint venture in Fuzhou (CIDA, 1984) the Chinese administer and finance housing, medical and welfare costs, the Japanese partner oversees the technical and production areas, and they jointly oversee hiring and firing.

A great deal of variability exists between the source of investment and the foreign equity percentage (Table 8.8). For example,

Table 8.7: Most frequently observed foreign equity percentages (n = 802)

50%	=	247
40%	=	97
25%	=	88
30%	=	71
49%	=	60

115

Hong Kong investors seem much more willing to take a minority equity position than investors from Europe, USA or Japan. Some Chinese officials will privately admit that desire for equal or majority ownership by European, Japanese and American firms contributed — at least in the early years — to their lower levels of investment. Yet as Schaan (1983) has pointed out in other developing countries, control is possible even with a minority equity position. Some of the control mechanisms available include use of contracts, the ability to set policies and procedures, staffing, and the design of the reporting structure.

Table 8.8: Foreign equity percentage, by country

%	Hong Kong	USA	Japan	Europe	Other	Total
< 40	227	14	12	5	11	269 (33.4%)
40–48	132	9	5	8	2	156 (19.4%)
49	44	8	4	2	2	60 (7.4%)
50	170	19	25	14	19	247 (30.6%)
> 50	55	6	8	1	3	73 (9.1%)
Total	628 (78.8%)	56 (7.0%)	54 (6.7%)	30 (3.7%)	37 (4.6%)	805 (100.0%)

For most Western firms the most unusual element of joint venturing in China is the use of a fade-out provision. As Table 8.9 demonstrates, over half of the JVs formed until 1985 were established in such a way that at the end of ten years, the entire business would become wholly Chinese-owned. Thus, rather than an indefinite stream of earnings, many foreign firms were forced to base their investment decision on a different set of assumptions.

The fade-out provision has made some multinationals nervous. They fear that if there are start-up delays or other unforeseen developments, they will be unable to recoup their total investment. Solutions do exist, of which the most frequently observed has been to extend the fade-out provision beyond ten years.

116

Table 8.9: Predetermined duration (in years) of JVs formed

	Frequency
2 9	113
10	357
11 14	54
16 20	85
21 60	41
Missing or unspecified	31
	840

8.4 CONCLUSION

The joint venture process in China is different. It is different from joint ventures in developed countries and different from joint ventures in developing countries which have market economies. These differences stem as much from politics as they do from the short time period in which the regulatory infrastructure has been enacted.

Much progress has been made and will continue to be made. The foreign investor contemplating the establishment of a JV in China now has a commercial code as a guide, can look forward to less uncertainty with respect to negotiations, and has historical data — some of which were presented here — to clarify what common practice has been.

Yet problems will also remain. There have been many more joint venture agreements signed than there are joint ventures in operation. In fact, *The Economist* (16th August 1986) noted that 'less than one-third of the 2,600 joint venture companies named so far have actually gone into business'. This is due to many factors including inflexibility, a short-term orientation, management problems and foreign exchange difficulties. At all times the foreign investors must keep in mind that a long-term, flexible attitude is needed. To overcome foreign exchange difficulties may require a willingness to consider some form of countertrade, something which many firms rightly consider unwieldy.

Multinationals which are patient, which offer China what it needs, and which are willing to reconsider some of the traditional methods it has used for doing business, can be successful investors. Such an approach will not be practical for all firms. Where such a profile does exist, the Chinese market will continue to hold much promise.

NOTE

*This chapter was co-authored by Hui Wang.

9

Joint Ventures in China: Legal Implications*

Nearly all of the foreign direct investment in the People's Republic of China has been through the joint-venture organisational form. The Chinese joint-venture laws governing such investment are quite distinct from those in other countries. Managers — not solely lawyers — in Western firms contemplating an equity joint-venture investment in China require familiarity with this legal system. This chapter presents a managerially oriented overview of recent developments in Chinese joint-venture law.

9.1 INTRODUCTION

With the Joint Venture Law (JVL)[1] of 1979, the People's Republic of China (PRC) began enacting laws and regulations to establish the institutional and legislative infrastructure urgently needed to encourage and facilitate the cooperation of foreign investors in its economic modernisation programme. Institutional changes[2] included the creation of organisations such as the China International Trust and Investment Corporation (CITIC), decentralisation of decision-making powers and the establishment of the Special Economic Zones (SEZs) in which foreign investors were granted preferential treatment and many principles of the free-market system govern. The success of the SEZ experience led to the granting of similar status to 14 coastal cities in May 1984 as a further incentive for foreign investment.

To acquire foreign technology, the PRC allows a wide variety of contractual forms including equity joint ventures, cooperative

119

enterprises, compensation trade and to a limited but increasing degree (primarily in the SEZs), wholly foreign-owned enterprises. The Chinese distinguish between equity joint ventures and cooperative enterprises (also referred to as contractual joint ventures). While the former is a limited liability company established under the JVL, the rights and obligations of the latter are governed by the negotiated contract. Most cooperative enterprises do not form an independent legal entity and profits, losses and risks are to be shared according to the contract.

The initial period following the promulgation of the JVL was disappointing for the PRC. Foreign investors preferred to use other forms of investment of a short-term nature. These did not demand the high degree of cooperation with Chinese partners as required by a joint venture. However, in 1983, a number of tax, tariff and other measures, including the enactment of the long-awaited Implementing Regulations[3] in September 1983, resulted in a dramatic increase in foreign investment in equity joint ventures.

In 1984 alone, over 740 joint venture agreements with a combined value of US $1.1 billion were approved. According to Yu Bo-Wei (1985) this was more than in the previous five years combined. Mega joint venture projects include the US $650 million contract for the development of a surface coal mine between China and Occidental Petroleum Corp signed on 29th June 1985 and the US $4 billion contract signed in January 1985 by the Guangdong Nuclear Power Investment Co and the Hong Kong Nuclear Investment Co.

Although legislation has been passed allowing for wholly-owned foreign enterprises, the PRC still considers the joint venture to be the investment form most suited to satisfy its development requirements. Given the preference of the PRC for the use of joint ventures, this chapter will highlight recent legislative developments affecting joint ventures, with particular emphasis on the Implementing Regulations.

9.2   THE IMPLEMENTING REGULATIONS

Establishment and approval

With over 400,000 individual enterprises, there is no lack of potential joint venture partners in China. Joint ventures can be arranged with many of these enterprises, provincial or regional groups or governments, and through the CITIC.

The joint venture is required to be established and governed exclusively by Chinese law. Despite substantial legislative advances in recent years, legislation has yet to be enacted in certain important areas. For example, there presently does not exist a corporation or bankruptcy act in China. It is therefore prudent to negotiate the terms of the joint venture contract to cover these deficiencies. At a minimum, the contents of the joint venture contract and the articles of association must meet the mandatory requirements listed in articles 14 and 15 of the Implementing Regulations. These requirements reflect standard contractual contents derived from various Western legal systems such as the names of the parties, the purpose of the business, total amount of investment, etc. In China, 'fade-out' joint ventures are frequently used. A pre-determined life for the joint venture — usually ten to 25 years — is set at the time of establishment (Table 8.9).

All joint ventures must normally be approved by the Ministry of Foreign Economic Relations and Trade. The approval authority may be transferred to provincial or municipal authorities if the investment amount is within the limit set by the State Council and if resources are not required to be allocated from other provinces. This has occurred in the special economic zones as well as in the coastal cities mentioned earlier. Eleven of these cities, for example, have approval power for projects of a total investment up to US $5 million, Dalian up to US $10 million and Shanghai and Tianjiin up to US $30 million.

Applicants must demonstrate that the venture will promote the socialist modernisation programme. Approval will be granted only on condition that the venture provides at least one of the following: 1) advanced technology and scientific management enabling an increase in the variety, quality and quantity of production and a saving of energy and materials; 2) technical renovation of enterprises resulting in less investment and increased profits; 3) emphasis on production of goods for export to increase foreign currency receipts; and 4) training of technical and managerial personnel. Once approved, the joint venture must register with the administrative bureau for industry and commerce of the province, municipality or region. The approval authority is further responsible for supervising and inspecting the joint venture's operation and approving all subsequent modifications of the contract or its appendices.

Given the developing nature of many industries in the PRC, it is worth noting that the most advanced technology may not be suitable for China's needs. Many non-technology-leading firms are unaware that they may already possess the most appropriate technology/process for China.

Capital contribution

While the foreign participant is generally required under the JVL to contibute a minimum of 25 per cent of the joint venture's capital, no maximum ceiling on its contribution is stipulated (Table 8.6). However, for tax considerations and since a majority equity position does not result in control of the venture, the foreign partner is usually content with a capital contribution of between 25 and 50 per cent (Pattison, 1981). This willingness to assume a minority position may in part be due to the persisting apprehension that the Chinese partner may act according to political rather than economic considerations or that the PRC will alter its favourable economic policies. Nonetheless, as Chapter 2 noted, a minority equity position for the foreign company is the most frequently observed equity level in other developing countries as well.

Contributions in kind (other than the right to use of a site) may be valued by joint assessment of the parties or the parties may agree upon a third party who will make the evaluation. If the right to use of a site is not included as part of the Chinese side's contribution, the joint venture shall pay annual rent for its use.

Contributions in kind by the foreign partner are subject to examination and approval of the approval authorities. In line with the policy of self-reliance, approval for machinery, equipment and other material, is granted only if it is indispensable to the joint venture's production and is incapable of being manufactured in China or manufactured only at an excessive price. Industrial property and know-how have to meet one of the following requirements. It has to be capable of: 1) producing new products which are 'urgently needed in China' or are suitable for export; 2) considerably improving the quality of existing goods as well as increasing productivity; or 3) effecting 'notable savings' in raw materials and energy. Extensive documentation relating to the industrial property or know-how, including legal certificates, technical characteristics and price calculations are annexed to the contract.

It is also possible for a foreign participant or a third party to transfer technology to the joint venture, separate from its capital contribution, by means of a technology transfer agreement. These contracts are governed by the Import of Technology Law of May 1985. Agreement and documentation are also subject to government approval. Payments are generally made in royalties, calculated on the basis of sales of products produced with the relevant technology.

The PRC has made significant advances in providing foreign investors with effective protection of their industrial property rights. In addition to recent legislation protecting trademarks and patent rights, China has signed bilateral treaties which grant such protection and has become a signatory to the Paris Convention for the Protection of Industrial Property, and a member of the World Intellectual Property Organisation (WIPO).

Control and management

Fundamental issues of the joint venture must, under the conditions of the contract, be discussed and acted upon by the board of directors. As Lussenburg (1985) has noted, the board of directors has broad management powers — but labour relations do not fall within the purview of its responsibilities. Guidance here is provided by the *Regulations on labour management on joint ventures using Chinese and foreign investment*.

Although the composition of the board is determined 'with reference to the proportion of investment contributed', control over operations is not ensured by majority equity ownership. Instead, decisions are made through 'consultation' of the parties, based on the 'principle of equity and mutual benefit'. Decisions to amend the articles of association, to terminate the venture, to increase or assign the registered capital or to merge with another economic organisation are required to be unanimously agreed upon by the directors. The rules of procedure set out in the articles of association of individual joint ventures often provide further minority protection by requiring that other major issues be decided by majority voting, which either implicitly or explicitly implies that a director from both

123

parties vote with the majority. Given the conflicting motivations of the parties, the potential for non-consensus is quite substantial and it is therefore essential that firms from the outset have confidence in the contribution of their partner and that the joint venture is the appropriate form to structure their investment.

Daily management is the responsibility of the management office whose powers, working rules and procedures are determined by the board of directors. Major decisions of this office require consultation between the general manager and the deputy general managers, positions which are normally divided between foreign and Chinese appointees. One arrangement that has found favour with the Chinese, is to provide for the rotation of management and mutual control, whereby each party appoints candidates who will alternate between the roles of general manager and deputy manager(s). If the foreign party appoints the general manager, the Chinese party has the right to appoint the chief accountant, and the chief auditor will be an appointee of the foreign venture. A suggested contractual requirement of a sample joint venture contract recently worked out by the Laws and Regulations Bureau of the Chinese Ministry of Foreign Economic Relations and Trade, demands further that major decisions should be signed jointly by the general manager and deputy general managers.[4] This again emphasises the desire of the Chinese for consultation and involvement at all levels of decision-making.

Planning, purchasing and selling

In order to integrate the joint venture into the central plan of the PRC, a capital construction plan as well as a production and operating plan are required to be formulated and filed with the department in charge of the joint venture. This not only aids in the distribution of domestic supplies, but it is also a source of information to ensure that the joint-venture operation complements the schemes of the central authorities.

Although materials may be purchased abroad, first priority should be given to Chinese suppliers where the 'conditions are the same'. The channels of supply and prices of the materials are also determined by the Regulations. Six raw materials (gold, silver, platinum, petroleum, coal and timber) used directly in production for export, are priced by the authorities. Prices for import or export commodities handled by Chinese foreign trade companies have to be negotiated and paid for in foreign currency while prices for other materials, utility and service fees are treated equally; their prices are paid by state-owned enterprises, in local currency (Renminbi).

To increase China's foreign currency earning, a joint venture is encouraged to export. Certainly access to the Southeast Asian market is one reason for interest in China. Products that are urgently needed in China may be sold on the Chinese market. The joint venture may export its products itself or it may entrust a foreign party or Chinese foreign trade corporations with export sales. The joint venture may also set the export price of its products.

For the Chinese domestic market, products which come under planned distribution arrangements must be sold by the joint venture to the authorities in charge of distribution. Any excess, together with materials that are not centrally distributed, may be sold directly by the joint venture, but prices have to correspond with state-set prices.

Methods of purchasing and selling and the ratio of products to be sold on the domestic market and on international markets are stipulated in the joint-venture contract. For items which require import or export licences, the joint venture is required to make import and export plans every year and apply semi-annually for these licences.

Taxation

An extensive tax regime[5] has been implemented by the PRC since the passing of the Joint Venture Law. Although a comprehensive analysis is beyond the scope of this book, the following outlines some of the major developments.

The tax rate for joint ventures is 33 per cent on net income, which includes a ten per cent local surtax. The income of a joint venture scheduled to operate for at least ten years, is exempt from taxation during its first two profit-making years. A further 50 per cent reduction is available for the following three years. These exemptions and reductions do not appear to be limited to joint ventures which are 'equipped with up-to-date technology by world standards', as initially contemplated by the JVL, although the PRC does grant certain industries favourable tax

125

rates. For example, joint ventures engaged in harbour construction are taxed at a rate of 15 per cent; they are exempt from tax during the first five years and are granted a 50 per cent reduction in the second five years (Yao, 1986).

A 40 per cent tax refund is available to a joint-venture participant that reinvests its share of profits into the joint venture or into other joint ventures in China for a minimum of five years. A ten per cent dividend tax is also levied on profits remitted out of China by a foreign party. No reduction or exemption of this tax is currently possible outside of the Special Economic Zones.

A 20 per cent withholding tax under the Foreign Enterprise Income Tax Law (FEITL) may apply to interest, rentals or technology fees paid to the foreign participant or a third party. This would apply to royalties or licence fees paid under ancillary agreements with the joint venture. This withholding tax may be reduced or exempted entirely for certain technology which is 'advanced' and offered at 'preferential terms'.

Joint ventures now are exempt from customs duty and Industrial and Commercial Consolidated Tax (ICCT) for machinery, equipment, parts and other materials imported as part of the foreign participant's capital contribution or as part of the joint venture's total investment or with additional capital upon authorisation, where the production and supply of the items cannot be guaranteed in China. Also exempted are raw materials, auxiliary materials, components, parts and packing materials imported for the production of export goods. Subject to the approval of the Ministry of Finance, ICCT does not apply to export sales, other than export items restricted by the state. Joint ventures that 'have difficulty' paying ICCT for an initial period of production on products sold domestically, may apply for a reduction or exemption of the tax.

Financial matters and foreign exchange

After-tax profits are distributed in proportion to each party's contribution but prior to distribution, allocations for reserve funds, bonuses and welfare funds for employees and expansion funds are deducted. The proportion of these allocations is determined by the board of directors.

Quarterly and annual accounts have to be submitted to the

partners, the local tax authorities, the department in charge of the joint venture and the financial authorities. The original approval authority also receives a set of the annual accounts because of its supervision role over the joint venture.

The Foreign Exchange Control Regulations require that all foreign exchange income from a joint venture be deposited in an account in the Bank of China (or in another approved bank) and that all foreign exchange obligations are made from this account. This includes payments for imported equipment and raw material, salaries of expatriate employees, royalties, interest on foreign loans and distribution of profits to the foreign participant. An imbalance in the foreign exchange account of a joint venture whose production has official approval to be sold primarily on the Chinese market, is made up from governmental foreign exchange reserves. This guarantee considerably enhances the prospects of joint ventures entering the immense domestic market.

Duration, dissolution and liquidation

Upon approval of all parties and approval of the examining and approval authority, a joint venture may, under certain circumstances, extend its duration to be prematurely dissolved. Circumstances for dissolution include heavy losses, major breach of contract by one of the parties, *'force majeure'*, or 'inability to obtain the desired objectives of the operation and at the same time to see a future for development'. The parties may provide for further reasons for dissolution in the joint-venture contract. A procedure for the appointment and activities of a liquidation committee are set out in the Implementing Regulations.

Dispute settlement and arbitration

Given the limited number of lawyers in China and the preference of the Chinese for a nonconfrontational process for dispute settlement, disputes arising in the execution of a joint-venture contract are to be settled primarily through 'friendly consultation' or conciliation. If these means are insufficient to resolve the dispute, the parties may resort to arbitration or litigation. However in recent years, conciliation has been the most

127

important mechanism for resolving international commercial disputes. In fact, a pronounced characteristic of the arbitration agencies in China is that they will strive for settlement by conciliation even after the dispute has been submitted to arbitration and the proceedings have commenced.

If the parties choose to apply for arbitration, they can do so in accordance with a written agreement. This agreement may be included in the joint-venture contract, or it may be entered into after the dispute has arisen. The forum, to be agreed upon by the parties, may be the Foreign Economic and Trade Arbitration Commission or an arbitration agency located in the defendant's country or one located in a third country. In each case, the procedural rules of the respective arbitration agency apply. With respect to substantive law, although the recent Economic Contract Law of the People's ·Republic of China Involving Foreigners allows international disputes over most commercial contracts to be settled according to the law of the parties' choice, joint-venture contracts are governed by the law of the PRC. In the absence of applicable legislation in China, 'international norms' apply. International treaties to which the PRC is a signatory prevail over conflicting Chinese legislation. If no written arbitration agreement exists between the parties, either side is free to file suit with the Chinese People's Republic Court.

9.3 CONCLUSION

Despite the considerable progress in establishing a modern legal system and the constitutional guarantee of the rights and interests of all foreign economic organisations operating in the PRC, many foreigners remain hesitant regarding investment in China. Although the decentralisation policy and the increased negotiating experience of the Chinese have reduced the time required for negotiation and approval of projects, many firms continue to view these periods as still too protracted to merit involvement in the PRC. Moreover, problems such as the underdeveloped infrastructure, a huge bureaucracy, and energy and exchange supply shortages further hinder the efficient progress of some joint ventures after operations have begun.

Whether or not the trend towards longer-term investment and in particular the use of joint ventures continues, will depend on the PRC's willingness to continue to improve its legal, taxation and planning systems. Recent developments demonstrating that the current Chinese leadership remains committed to this policy should therefore encourage optimism amongst foreign investors.

NOTES

*This chapter was co-authored by Terrance Conley. An earlier version appeared in *Business Quarterly* (November 1986), Vol. 51, No. 3, pp. 39–43 and is reproduced with permission.

1. Law of the People's Republic of China on Joint Ventures Using Chinese and Foreign Investment, enacted on 1st July 1979 and promulgated 8th July 1979 (hereinafter cited as JVL).

2. For an examination of the institutional changes, see Alford and Birenbaum (1981) and Kueh and Howe (1984).

3. Regulations for the Implementation of the Law of the People's Republic of China on Joint Ventures Using Chinese and Foreign Investment, promulgated on 20th September 1983 (hereinafter cited as Implementing Regulations).

4. Sample Articles of Association for Joint Ventures Using Chinese and Foreign Investment, *China Economic News*, No. 4 (1st April 1985), art. 34.

5. Income Tax Law of the People's Republic of China Concerning Joint Ventures Using Chinese and Foreign Investment, adopted on 10th September 1980 (hereinafter cited as JVITL); Detailed Rules and Regulations for the Implementation of the Income Tax Law of the People's Republic of China Concerning Joint Ventures Using Chinese and Foreign Investment, promulgated on 14th December 1980 (hereinafter cited as JVITL Rules). Further developments in the Chinese tax field include tax treaties recently signed with the United Kingdom, Japan, the United States, France, Germany and Canada concerning the avoidance of double taxation.

Appendix 1

PARTIAL LIST OF FIRMS CONTACTED

ACCO
American Cyanamid
Brascan
Canada Packers
Canada Wire and Cable
Canadian Overseas Packaging Industries
C.I.L.
Diversey-Wyandotte
Emco-Wheaton
Heinemann
Imperial Optical
Labatt's
Maple Leaf Mills
Massey-Ferguson
Mentholatum
Moore Business Forms
Noranda
Northern Telecom
Pillsbury
Standard Brands
Sterling Drugs

Appendix 2

MANAGEMENT CASE STUDIES OF JOINT VENTURES IN LDCs

	Written	Period covered	Countries	Issue	Length	Author	Case distributor
Maple Leaf Tobacco (B)	1982	1979	Canada-LDC	JV redesign Ownership % of problem JV	21pp.	T. A. Poynter	UWO[1]
Ampak	1974	1975	USA-Pakistan	Assessing a partner	11pp	Springate	Author
Dykins	1982	1982	Canada/UK/LDCs	Growth	23pp	H. W. Lane	UWO
Nike (in China)	1985	1984	US-China	Ongoing management	37pp	F. J. Aguilar	Harvard
Nike (in China — 1985)	1986	1985	US-China	Managing a JV in China	15pp	F. J. Aguilar	Harvard
Canada Royal (Int'l) (A)	1982	1977	Canada-Latin America	Entire JV process	15pp	H. W. Lane	UWO
Canada Royal (Int'l) (B)	1982	1982	Canada-Latin America	Entire JV process	26pp	H. W. Lane	UWO
Parker Hannifin (in China) (A)	1982	1980	US-China	Proposed JV in China	33pp	D. D. Wyckoff and J. R. Williams	Harvard

	Written	Period covered	Countries	Issue	Length	Author	Case distributor
Parker Hannifin (in China) (B)	1982	1981	US-China	Description of agreement	9pp	D. D. Wyckoff and J. R. Williams	Harvard
Scott Paper Int'l	1980	1978	US-Korea	Proposed JV	46pp	C. B. Malone	Harvard
Daewoo Group	1984	1984	Korea (US)	Growth by collaborative arrangements	20pp	F. J. Aguilar	Harvard
Ssangyong-Scott	1981	1980	US-Korea	Marketing issues in a start-up JV	26pp	C. B. Malone	Harvard
Larson	1980	1979	Canada-Nigeria	Indigenisation	6pp	I. A. Litvak	Author
Two-Ply Manufactures	1971	1971	US-Ivory Coast-Mexico	Assessing troublesome JVs	10pp	L. J. Wells	Harvard
Minneapolis Foods (JV in Guatemala)	1983	1982	US-LDC	Merging the expertise of JV partners	6pp	W. Renforth	Author
Ulker Biscuits, Inc	1983	1983	Turkey, Middle East	Alternative market-entry strategies	6pp	E. Kaynak	Author
Corning Glass Works	1984	1979	Us-Indonesia	Proposed JV	24pp	M. Y. Yoshino	Harvard
Honeywell, Inc. (in Brazil)	1985	1985	US-Brazil	Selecting local partner	31pp	D. C. Hastings	Minnesota

Note 1. University of Western Ontario.

Bibliography

Adler, Lee and Hlavacek, James D. (1976) *Joint ventures for product innovation*, Amacom, New York

Aharoni, Yair (1966) *The foreign investment decision process*, Harvard University Press, Boston, Massachusetts

Alexrod, R. M. (1984) *The evolution of cooperation*, Basic Books, New York

Alford, W. P. and Birenbaum, D. E. (1981) 'Ventures in China trade: an analysis of China's emerging legal framework for the regulation of foreign investment', *Northwestern Journal of International Law and Business* 56

Artisien, Patrick F. R. and Buckley, Peter J. (1985) 'Joint ventures in Yugoslavia: opportunities and constraints', *Journal of International Business Studies*, spring, 1, pp. 111–36

Baetz, Mark C. and Beamish, Paul W. (1987) *Strategic management: Canadian cases*, Richard D. Irwin, Homewood, Illinois

Beamish, Paul W. (1984) 'Joint venture performance in developing countries', unpublished doctoral dissertation, University of Western Ontario, London, Ontario

—— (1984) 'The long march to China trade', *Policy Options*, Vol. 5, No. 6, November, pp. 30–3

—— (1985) 'The characteristics of joint ventures in developed and developing countries', *Columbia Journal of World Business*, winter, pp. 13–19

—— (1987) 'Joint ventures in LDCs: partner selection and performance', *International Management Review*, Vol. 27, I, pp. 23–37

—— and Carr-Harris, Hugh (1984) 'High-tech road to China', *Canadian Export World*, Vol. 1, No. 5, December, pp. 35–6

—— and Tan, Wei Wen (1985) 'Improving Canadian-Chinese economic ties', *Proceedings of the Southeast Asia Region of the Academy of International Business*, Hong Kong, July

—— and Barki, Henri (1986) 'International development through joint ventures: the role of commitment', *Proceedings of the International Conference on Marketing and Development*, Istanbul, Turkey, pp. 283–92

—— and Banks, John C. (1987) 'Equity joint ventures and the theory of the multinational enterprise', *Journal of International Business Studies*, summer, pp. 1–16

—— and Lane, Henry W. (1987) 'Implementing joint ventures in developing countries', Working Paper 86–06 (revised), School of Business Administration, University of Western Ontario

Berg, Sanford V. and Friedman, Philip (1978, 1979) 'Joint ventures in American industry', parts I, II, III, *Mergers and Acquisitions*, summer 1978, autumn, 1978, winter 1979.

134

—— (1980) 'Corporate courtship and successful joint ventures', *California Management Review*, spring, Vol. 22, No. 3, pp. 85–91

Berlew, F. Kingston (1984) 'The joint venture — a way into foreign markets', *Harvard Business Review*, July–August

Bivens, K. K. and Lovell, E. B. (1966) *Joint ventures with foreign partners*, Conference Board, New York

Brams, S. J. and Kilgour, Marc D. (1985) 'Optimal deterrence', *Social Philosophy and Policy*, Vol. 3, No. 1, pp. 118–35

Buckley, Peter J. (1985) 'New forms of international industrial cooperation', in Peter J. Buckley and Mark Casson (eds), *The economic theory of the multinational enterprise*, St Martin's Press, New York

—— and Casson, Mark (1976) *The future of the multinational enterprise*, Macmillan, London

—— (1985) *The economic theory of the multinational enterprise*, St Martin's Press, New York

—— (1987) 'A theory of cooperation in international business', in Farok J. Contractor and Peter Lorange (eds), *Cooperative strategies in international business*, D. C. Heath, Lexington, Massachusetts

Burton, F. N. and Saelens, F. H. (1982) 'Partner choice and linkage characteristics of international joint ventures in Japan: an exploratory analysis of the inorganic chemicals sector', *Management International Review*, Vol. 22, pp. 20–9

Business International, (1980) *201 checklists: decision-making in international operations*, March, pp. 56–62 ('Joint venture checklists: 44–50')

Calvet, A. L. (1981) 'A synthesis of foreign direct investment theories and theories of the multinational firm', *Journal of International Business Studies*, spring–summer, pp. 43–59

Canada Wire and Cable (1981) 'International joint ventures: Basic steps to follow in establishing a successful operation', Canadian International Development Agency (brochure) Ottawa, Canada

Canadian Consulate-General in Brazil (1981) *Joint business ventures in Brazil: a Canadian perspective*, Department of Industry, Trade and Commerce, Government of Canada, Ottawa, April

Cantwell, J. A. and Dunning, John H. (1984) 'The new forms of international involvement of British firms in the third world', Proceedings of the European International Business Association

Casson, Mark (1979) *Alternatives to the multinational enterprise*, Holmes and Meier, New York

—— (1982) 'Transaction costs and the theory of the multinational enterprise', in Alan M. Rugman (ed.), *New theories of the multinational enterprise*, Croom Helm, London and St Martin's Press, New York

Caves, Richard E. (1982) *Multinational enterprise and economic analysis*, Cambridge University Press, Cambridge, Massachusetts

China International Economic Consultants, Inc (1985, 1986) *China Investment Guide*, Longmans, London

Coase, Ronald H. (1952) 'The nature of the firm', *Economica* (1937): 386–405; reprinted in *Readings in price theory*, G. Stigler and K. Boulding (eds), Irwin, Homewood, Illinois

Cohen, Jerome Alan (1982) 'Equity joint ventures: 20 potential pitfalls that every company should know about', *The China Business Review*, November–December, pp. 23–30
—— (ed.) (1983) *Legal aspects of doing business in China*, Practising Law Institute, New York
Coish, H. O. (1981) 'Joint ventures and bilateral trade agreements', *Canada Commerce*, January
Conley, Terrance W. (1985) 'Recent developments in Chinese joint-venture law', unpublished mimeograph, Bielefeld, West Germany
—— and Beamish, Paul W. (1986) 'Joint ventures in China: legal implications', *Business Quarterly*, November, Vol. 51, No. 3, pp. 39–43
Consult Asia Inc, 'A guide to technology transfers to the People's Republic of China', Canadian International Development Agency, September 1984, pp. 19–20
Contractor, Farok J. (1985) 'A generalised theorem for joint-venture and licensing negotiations', *Journal of International Business Studies*, summer, 2, pp. 23–50
—— and Lorange, Peter (1987) *Cooperative strategies in international business*, D. C. Heath, Lexington, Massachusetts
Cory, Peter F. (1982) 'Industrial cooperation, joint ventures and the MNE in Yugoslavia', in Alan M. Rugman (ed.), *New theories of the multinational enterprise*, Croom Helm, London and St Martin's Press, New York
Cozzolino, John M. (1981) 'Joint venture risk: how to determine your share', *Mergers and Acquisitions*, autumn
Dang, Tran (1977) 'Ownership, control and performance of the multinational corporation: a study of US wholly-owned subsidiaries and joint ventures in the Philippines and Taiwan', unpublished Ph.D. dissertation, University of California
Daniels, John D., Krug, Jeffrey and Nigh, Douglas (1985) 'US joint ventures in China: motivation and management of political risk', *California Management Review*, summer, pp. 46–58
Davidson, William H. and McFetridge, Donald G. (1985) 'Key characteristics in the choice of international technology transfer mode', *Journal of International Business Studies*, summer, 2, pp. 5–21
Dunning, John H. (1958) *American investment in British manufacturing industry*, George Allen and Unwin, London
—— (1981) *International production and the multinational enterprise*, George Allen and Unwin, London
—— (1985) 'The eclectic paradigm of international production: an update and a reply to its critics', unpublished mimeograph, Department of Economics, University of Reading
The Economist (1986) 'Joint ventures in China: after the honeymoon', 16th August, pp. 4–8
Encarnation, Dennis J. (1982) 'The political economy of Indian joint industrial ventures abroad', *International Organization*, Vol. 36, No. 1, winter
Franko, Lawrence G. (1971) 'Joint venture divorce in the multinational company', *Columbia Journal of World Business*, May–June

—— (1971) *Joint venture survival in multinational corporations*, Praeger, New York

—— (1972) 'The art of choosing an American joint venture partner', in Michael Z. Brooke and H. Lee Remmers (eds), *The multinational company in Europe*, Longman, London, pp. 67–76

—— (1976) *The European multinationals*, Harper and Row, New York

—— (1986) 'New forms of investment in developing countries: practices of US companies', May 1985 paper included in *The proceedings of the cooperative strategies in international business colloquium*, F. Contractor and P. Lorange (eds), Rutgers, New Jersey, October

Friedmann, Wolfgang G. and Beguin, J. P. (1971) *Joint international business ventures in developing countries*, Columbia Univeristy Press, New York

—— and Kalmanoff, George (1961) *Joint international business ventures*, Columbia University Press, New York

—— and Mates, Leo (1968) *Joint business ventures of Yugoslav enterprises and foreign firms*, Belgrade

Geringer, J. Michael (1986) 'Criteria for selecting partners for joint ventures in industrialised market economies', unpublished PhD dissertation, University of Washington, State of Washington

Ginzberg, M. J. (1981) 'Key recurrent issues in the MIS implementation process', *MIS Quarterly*, June, pp. 47–59

Gullander, Staffan (1976) 'Joint ventures and corporate strategy', *Columbia Journal of World Business*, spring, pp. 104–14

—— (1976) 'Joint ventures in Europe: determinants of entry', *International Studies of Management and Organization*, Vol. 6, No. 1–2, spring–summer

Hampton, G. M. and Van Gent, A. P. (1984) *Marketing aspects of international business*, Kluwer-Nijhoff, Boston, Massachusetts

Harrigan, Kathryn Rudie (1984) 'Joint ventures and global strategies', *Columbia Journal of World Business*, Vol. 19, No. 2, summer, pp. 7–16

—— (1985) *Strategies for joint ventures*, D. C. Heath, Lexington, Maryland

Hendryx, Steven R. (1986) 'The China trade — making the deal work', *Harvard Business Review*, July–August, pp. 75, 81–4

Hennart, Jean-François (1982) *A theory of multinational enterprise*, University of Michigan Press, Ann Arbour

—— (1985) 'What is internalisation?', unpublished mimeograph, The Wharton School, Philadelphia, Pennsylvania

Hills, Stephen M. (1978) 'The search for joint venture partners', *Academy of Management Proceedings*, pp. 277–81

Horstmann, Ignatius and Markusen, James R. (1986) 'Licensing versus direct investment: a model of internationalisation by the multinational enterprise', unpublished mimeograph, Department of Economics, University of Western Ontario, London, Ontario, March

Hymer, Stephen (1973) 'Comment by Stephen Hymer (on "Effects of

policies encouraging foreign joint ventures in developing countries''
by Louis T. Wells)', in Ayal, E. (ed.), *Micro aspects of development*,
Praeger, New York
—— (1976) *The international operations of national firms: a study of
direct foreign investment*, MIT Press, Cambridge, Massachusetts
International Management (1984) 'Should the CEO proceed with his
joint-venture plans?', May
Janger, Allen R. (1980) *Organisation of international joint ventures*,
The Conference Board, New York
Killing, J. Peter (1978) 'Joint venture stability', Working Paper 211,
School of Business Administration, University of Western Ontario,
London, Ontario, October
—— (1980) 'Technology acquisition: Licence agreement or joint
venture', *Columbia Journal of World Business*, autumn, pp. 38–46
—— (1982) 'How to make a global joint venture work', *Harvard
Business Review*, May–June, pp. 120–7
—— (1983) *Strategies for joint venture success*, Praeger, New York
Kobayashi, Noritake (1967) 'Some organisational problems', in R. T.
Ballon (ed.), *Joint ventures and Japan* (Part 3), Sophia University,
Tokyo
Kogut, Bruce (1987) 'Joint ventures: a review and preliminary investiga-
tion', in Farok J. Contractor and Peter Lorange (eds), *Cooperative
strategies in international business*, D. C. Heath, Lexington,
Maryland
Kolde, E. J. (1974) *The multinational company*, Lexington Books,
Toronto
Kueh, Y. Y. and Howe, Christopher (1984) 'China's international
trade: policy and organisational change and their place in the
economic readjustment', *The China Quarterly*, 100
Lecraw, Donald J. (1983) 'Performance of transnational corporations
in less developed countries', *Journal of International Business
Studies*, spring–summer, pp. 15–34
Lussenburg, Selma M. (1985) 'Joint venture investments in the People's
Republic of China: a continuing challenge', *The Canadian Bar
Review*, 63, September, pp. 546–96
Matthews, Geoffrey J. and Morrow, Robert, Jr (1985) *Canada and the
world: an atlas resource*, Prentice-Hall, Scarborough, Ontario
Mergers and Acquisitions (1983) 'Mergers and corporate policy', in
'Joint venture rosters'
—— (1972–6) 'Joint venture rosters', Vols. 72–76
Mintzberg, H. (1980) *The nature of managerial work*, Prentice-Hall,
Englewood Cliffs, New Jersey
McMillan, C. H. and St Charles, D. P. (1974) *Joint ventures in
eastern Europe: a three-country comparison*, C. D. Howe Research
Institute, Montreal
Nunnally, J. C. (1967, 1978), *Psychometric theory*, McGraw-Hill,
Toronto
Nehemkis, Peter and Nehemkis, Alexis (1980) 'China's law on joint
ventures', *California Management Review*, summer, Vol. 22, No. 4,
pp. 37–46

Newbould, Gerald D., Buckley, Peter J. and Thurwell, Jane C. (1978) *Going international*, John Wiley and Sons, Toronto

Parry, Thomas G. (1985) 'Internalisation as a general theory of foreign direct investment: a critique', *Weltwirtschaftliches Archiv*, September

Pattison, J. E. (1981) 'China's developing legal framework for foreign investment: experience and expectations', *Law and Policy in International Business*, 89

Patton, Donald J. and Do, Anh-Dung (1978) 'Joint ventures in Yugoslavia', *Management International Review*, pp. 51-63

Peter, P. J. (1979) 'Reliability: a review of psychometric basics and recent marketing practices', *Journal of Marketing Research*, February

Peterson, Richard B. and Shimada, Justin Y. (1978) 'Sources of management problems in Japanese-American joint ventures', *Academy of Management Review*, October, pp. 796-804

Poynter, Thomas A. (1982) 'Government intervention in less developed countries: the experience of multinational companies', *Journal of International Business Studies*, spring-summer, pp. 9-25

——— (1985) *Multinational enterprise and government intervention*, St Martin's Press, New York

Pye, Lucian W. (1986) 'The China trade: making the deal', *Harvard Business Review*, July-August, pp. 74, 76-80

Rafii, Farshad (1978) 'Joint ventures and transfer of technology to Iran: the impact of foreign control', unpublished Doctoral dissertation, Harvard University, Boston, Massachusetts

Raveed. S. R. and Renforth, W. (1983) 'State enterprise — multinational corporation joint ventures: how well do they meet both partners' needs?', *Management International Review*, Vol. 1, No. 1, pp. 47-57

Reynolds, John I. (1979) *Indian-American joint ventures: business policy relationships*, University Press of America, Washington, DC

——— (1984) 'The pinched-shoe effect of international joint ventures', *Columbia Journal of World Business*, Vol. 19, No. 2, summer, pp. 23-9

Riddle, Dorothy I. (1983) 'Reflections on the Asian perspective: joint ventures with the Japanese', unpublished mimeograph, May

Robock, S. H. and Simmonds, K. (1983) *International business and multinational enterprises*, third edition, Irwin, Homewood, Illinois

Roulac, Stephen E. (1980) 'Structuring the joint venture', *Mergers and Acquisitions*, spring

Rugman, Alan M. (1979) *International diversification and the multinational enterprise*, D. C. Heath, Lexington, Massachusetts

——— (1981) *Inside the multinationals: the economics of internal markets*, Croom Helm, London and Columbia University Press, New York

——— (1983) 'The comparative performance of US and European multinational enterprises 1970-9', *Management International Review*, 23, pp. 4-14

——— (1985) 'Internalisation is still a general theory of foreign direct investment', *Weltwirtschaftliches Archiv*, September

Saham, J. (1980) *British industrial investment in Malaysia — 1963 – 71*, Oxford University Press, Kuala Lumpur

Salancik, Gerald R. (1977) 'Commitment and the control of organisational behaviour and belief', in Barry M. Staw and Gerald R. Salancik, *New Directions in Organisational Behaviour*, St Clair Press, Chicago

Schaan, Jean-Louis (1983) 'Parent control and joint venture success: the case of Mexico', unpublished Doctoral dissertation, University of Western Ontario, London, Ontario

—— and Beamish, Paul W. (1987) 'Joint venture general managers in developing countries', in Farok Contractor and Peter Lorange (eds), *Cooperative Strategies in International Business*, D.C. Heath, Lexington, Massachusetts

Simyar, Farhad (1983) 'Major causes of joint-venture failures in the Middle East: the case of Iran', *Management International Review*, vol. 23, pp. 58 – 68

State Council (1983) 'Regulations for the implementation of the law of the People's Republic of China on joint ventures using Chinese and foreign investment', *Beijing Review*, No. 41, 10th October

Stevens, J. Hugh (1974) 'Joint ventures in Latin America', *The Business Quarterly*, winter, pp. 66 – 71

Stopford, John M. and Wells, Louis T., Jr (1972) *Managing the multinational enterprise*, Basic Books, New York

Stopford, J. M., Dunning, John H. and Haberich, Klaus O. (1980) *The world directory of multinational enterprises*, Facts on File Inc, New York

Stuckey, John A. (1983) *Vertical integration and joint ventures in the aluminum industry*, Harvard University Press, Cambridge, Massachusetts

Sullivan, Jeremiah and Peterson, Richard B. (1982) 'Factors associated with trust in Japanese-American joint ventures', *Management International Review*, Vol. 22, pp. 30 – 40

Teece, David J. (1981) 'The multinational enterprise: market failure and market power considerations', *Sloan Management Review*, spring, pp. 3 – 17

—— (1983) 'Multinational enterprise, internal governance and industrial organisation', *The American Economic Review*, Vol. 75, No. 2, May, pp. 233 – 8

Thorelli, Hans B. (1986) 'Networks: between markets and hierarchies', *Strategic Management Journal*, Vol. 7, pp. 37 – 51

Tomlinson, James W. C. (1970) *The joint venture process in international business: India and Pakistan*, MIT Press, Cambridge, Massachusetts

—— and Willie, C. S. W. (1982) 'Modelling the joint venture process in Latin America: Mexico', *Canadian Journal of Development Studies*, Vol. 3, No. 1

United Nations (1971) *Manual on the establishment of industrial joint-venture agreements in developing countries*, UN, New York

Vaupel, James W. and Curhan, Joan P. (1973) *The world's multi-*

national enterprises, Harvard University Press, Boston, Massachusetts

Walls, Jan (1986) 'The cultural context of communication in China: cross-cultural business skills', *Issues*, Asia Pacific Foundation of Canada, spring, pp. 1–7

Walmsley, John (1979) *Joint ventures in Saudi Arabia*, Graham and Trotman, London

――― (1982) *Handbook of international joint ventures*, Graham and Trotman, London

Wang, Hui Y. (1986) 'China sets up joint venture overseas', *Intertrade*, January

Wells, Louis T., Jr (1973) 'Joint ventures — successful handshake or painful headache?', *European Business*, summer, pp. 73–9

――― (1973) 'Effects of policies encouraging foreign joint ventures in developing countries', in Ayal, E. (ed.), *Micro aspects of development*, Praeger, New York

――― (1983) *Third world multinationals: the rise of foreign investment from developing countries*, MIT Press, Cambridge, Massachusetts

Williamson, Oliver E. (1975) *Markets and hierarchies: analysis and antitrust implications — a study in the economics of internal organisations*, Free Press, New York

――― (1983) 'Credible commitments: using hostages to support exchange', *The American Economic Review*, Vol. 73, No. 4, September, pp. 519–40

Wright, Richard W. and Russel, Colin S. (1975) 'Joint ventures in developing countries: realities and responses', *Columbia Journal of World Business*, summer, 74–80

――― (1981) 'Canadian joint ventures in Japan', in K. C. Dhawan, Hamid Etemad and Richard W. Wright (eds), *International business: a Canadian perspective*, Addison-Wesley, Don Mills, Ontario

――― (1981) 'Evolving international business arrangements', in K. C. Dhawan, Hamid Etemad and Richard W. Wright (eds), *International business: a Canadian perspective*, Addison-Wesley, Don Mills, Ontario

Yao, Zhuang (1986), *Lecture VI, 86–7*, Laws on Chinese-foreign joint ventures, University of East Asia, Macau, August

Yu Bo-wei (1985) 'International business prospects for China', Proceedings of the inaugural meeting of the Southeast Asia region, Academy of International Business, Hong Kong

Index

142

exports from JVs 8, 38, 85,
122, 125

fade out JVs 3, 94, 116
Finland 2
Fortune 500 1
France 75, 129
Franko, Lawrence G. 1, 2, 12,
13, 24
Friedman, Philip 17, 98
Friedmann, Wolfgang G. 24
Fujian-Hitachi Television
115

Game Theory 108
general managers
need for 25, 34
role of 51–4, 72–93
General Motors 1
Geringer, J. Michael 16, 20, 43,
60, 62
Germany 129
Ginzberg, M. J. 45, 46
government
frequency of government
partners 15, 22, 110–17
needs 26, 31, 33, 35
performance of government
partners 13, 42, 61
pressure from 12
Guangdon Nuclear Power
Investment Co. 120
guile 98, 100
Gullander, Staffan 12

Harrigan, Kathryn Rudie 1, 10,
97
Hennart, Jean-Francois 95, 96
Hills, Stephen M. 26
Hong Kong and Macao 112–16
Hong Kong Nuclear Investment
Co. 120
Horstmann, Ignatius 94
Howe, Christopher 129
human resource needs 25

independent JVs 20
India 14, 90
internalisation theory 94–109

Janger, Allen R. 1, 12, 13, 20,
26, 102, 103
Japan 2, 113, 114, 116, 129

Kilgour, Marc D. 108
Killing, J. Peter 11–13, 16,
18–21, 24, 26, 97, 102,
103
knowledge needs 26, 27
Kogut, Bruce 13, 108
Kolb-Frohman model of change
46
Kolde, E. J. 102
Kueh, Y. Y. 129

labour costs 31
Lane, Henry W. 6, 71
Latin America 6, 44, 62, 84
lawyers/legal perspective 6, 65,
90, 98, 101, 111, 119–29
leakage of proprietary
knowledge 101
licensing 1
Lorange, Peter 1
Lussenburg, Selma M. 123

management by objective 59
market access needs 12, 26
market share 8
Markusen, James R. 94
matrix structures 65
Matthews, Geoffrey J. 2
McFetridge, Donald G. 94, 96
mergers and acquisitions 1, 16,
17
Mexico 2, 6, 18, 20, 75,
84, 86–8
mining ventures 3, 13
Mintzberg, H. 72–4
MIS (Management Information
Systems) 4, 45
monopoly 8, 76, 99
Morrow, Robert 2
mutual forbearance 98

need for one's partner
literature 24, 25
measurement 28
typology 25–7
Newbould, Gerald D. 26